JOHN SKELTON

A SELECTION FROM HIS POEMS

A SERIES OF ENGLISH TEXTS

General Editor: Vivian de Sola Pinto, M.A., D.Phil.

JOHN SKELTON

A SELECTION FROM HIS POEMS

EDITED WITH AN INTRODUCTION BY

VIVIAN DE SOLA PINTO

M.A., D.Phil.

*Professor of English in the University
of Nottingham*

LONDON

SIDGWICK & JACKSON, LTD.

First Issued 1950

PRINTED AND BOUND IN GREAT BRITAIN BY
WILLIAM CLOWES AND SONS, LIMITED, LONDON AND BECCLES

PREFATORY NOTE

THE text of the poems in this selection is based on that of Dyce's great edition of 1847, which has been collated with the sixteenth-century editions listed in the Select Bibliography. No attempt has been made to give all the variant readings, but a few of the most significant have been recorded in the footnotes.

In accordance with the general plan of the series, the spelling has been modernized, except where old spellings have an aesthetic or philological value. Thus a spelling like " woundersly " has been changed to " wondrously ", but a spelling like " widerèd " for " withered " has been retained because it indicates the contemporary pronunciation and rhymes with the obsolete word " shiderèd " in the next line. The final e (or es) in Skelton's works presents difficulties. Sometimes it was certainly pronounced and at others it seems to have been mute. Where pronunciation of this letter seems necessary for rhythm or rhyme a dot has been placed over it. An accent has also been placed on syllables stressed in Skelton's time which are not accented in modern English.

Where only a part of a poem has been printed, the word " extract " is inserted below the title, and where omissions have been made, they are indicated by asterisks. Words are explained in the notes only on the first occasion on which they occur in the Selection. If an obsolete word is not explained in a footnote, it should be looked up in the Index to the Notes, which will indicate the page on which the explanation is given.

For the introduction and notes I am greatly indebted to Dyce's edition and to Professor Ian Gordon's invaluable monograph. I also wish to express my thanks to my colleague Miss Alice Selby for the considerable help which I have received from her in the preparation of the notes and to my old friend Mr. J. Isaacs, who has read the manuscript of the Introduction, and to whose delightful broadcast talk on Skelton I owe several suggestions.

V. DE SOLA PINTO.

NOTTINGHAM,
  1950.

CONTENTS

		PAGE
Prefatory Note		V
Introduction		1
Selections from Skelton's Poems		15
I	Of the Death of the Noble Prince Edward the Fourth	15
II	Upon a dead man's head	18
III	Lullay	21
IV	Woefully Arrayed	22
V	The Bowge of Court	25
VI	Philip Sparrow	44
VII	The Tunning of Elinour Rumming	72
VIII	Against the Scots	78
IX	Against Garnesche	80
X	From *Magnificence*	
	1. Fancy's Hawk	83
	2. Adversity Speaks	84
	3. Liberty's Song	85
	4. Goodhope and Magnificence	86
XI	Colin Clout	88
XII	Speak Parrot	98
XIII	Why Come Ye Not to Court?	104

PAGE

XIV From *The Garland of Laurel*
    1. To the right noble Countess of Surrey 110
    2. To Mistress Margery Wentworth 111
    3. To Mistress Isabel Pennell 112
    4. To Mistress Margaret Hussey 113
    5. To Mistress Isabel Knight 114

XV *The Duke of Albany* 116

XVI *A Defence of Poetry* (extract from *A Replication*) 119

BIBLIOGRAPHY 121

INDEX TO NOTES 123

INTRODUCTION

I

JOHN SKELTON is a poet whose genius is only beginning
to receive due recognition. He lived and wrote in an age
which was " between two worlds, one dead, the other
powerless to be born ". One world was the feudal and
Catholic civilization of the Middle Ages, which was
dying out at the opening of the sixteenth century ; the
other was the new humanist and individualist civilization,
which was painfully struggling into existence. Skelton
belongs to both worlds, and is, nevertheless, too original
to be considered as a typical representative of either.
As Professor Gordon has written, " he does not fit too
comfortably into a history of English Literature divided
into schools and periods, and he has been shuffled into an
obscure position far below his real merits ". Immediately
after him came the new school of courtier-poets, Sir
Thomas Wyatt and the Earl of Surrey, who brought to
England the Petrarchan convention of love poetry and
paved the way for the great Elizabethans. They laid the
foundations of the poetry of good manners, the " liquid
diction, the fluid movement " embodied in the work of
Spenser and his successors down to Tennyson and
Bridges. Skelton's best work represents another tradition, the popular tradition of supple, colloquial verse with
that " spring, bounding swiftness " which Arnold found
in Burns. This is a tradition which has never wholly
died out, but which was considered to be outside the pale
of " polite " literature for centuries.

Puttenham in his *Arte of English Poesie* (1589)
dismisses Skelton as " a rude rayling rimer " ; for
Pope (*Epistle to Augustus*, 1737) he is merely " beastly
Skelton " ; while Thomas Warton in his *History of
English Poetry* (1774–81) wrote that " Skelton would have

been a writer without decorum at any period ". Yet Skelton was never quite forgotten. John Hall, the Elizabethan satirist, mentions his " breath-lesse rimes ", Ben Jonson and Michael Drayton both experimented in " Skeltonic " metre, and an anonymous editor of 1718 praised his " just and natural description of those merry Wassail Days ". In 1843 Alexander Dyce produced his monumental edition of Skelton's *Poetical Works*, and Elizabeth Barrett Browning praised his poetry eloquently and acutely in her *Book of the Poets* (1863).

It was not, however, until the second decade of the present century that Skelton began to be recognized as one of the most interesting and important English poets between Chaucer and Shakespeare. He appealed to poets and critics of the twentieth century as an anti-romantic with a temper akin to their own, a deflater of pomposity, a writer with a clear, precise vision of the physical world who avoided cloudy generalities, and a highly original metrist whose verse is based on the rhythms of common speech rather than on rigid metrical patterns. Robert Graves has used the Skeltonic metre extensively and has praised Skelton in a notable poem. Echoes of Skeltonic rhythms are to be heard in T. S. Eliot's *Murder in the Cathedral* and in many poems of W. H. Auden, who has written an excellent essay on this " conservative cleric with a strong sense of humour", to whose nimble, pithy verse his own probably owes a considerable debt.

II

Skelton was born about 1460. He grew up in one of the most troubled periods of English history. The great house of Plantagenet, the centre of the English feudal monarchy, had split into two opposing branches, headed respectively by the saintly but feeble Henry VI and the vigorous, unscrupulous Yorkist princes. The English empire in France crumbled away, leaving only the single bastion of Calais, and the long dynastic wars dragged on till 1485, when Henry of Richmond won the Battle of Bosworth Field and established the new monarchy of the Tudors.

The place of Skelton's birth is unknown, but there is some reason to believe that it was in Norfolk, then one of the most prosperous parts of England and a great centre of the wool trade. He studied at Cambridge and probably also at Oxford and Louvain. Both Oxford and Cambridge granted him the title of *poeta laureatus*, which at that date was an academic degree involving a prolonged study of Latin grammar and rhetoric. His earliest known poem is an elegy on the Yorkist King Edward IV, who died in 1483. He produced translations of Cicero's letters and of the History of Diodorus Siculus, and he was highly complimented by Caxton in the prologue to his *Boke of the Eneydos* (1490) both for his classical learning and for his translations of Latin authors into " polyshed and ornate termes ". At the request of Henry VII he became tutor to the young princes Arthur and Henry (afterwards Henry VIII). He was now an important person in courtly and academic circles, and seems to have been granted a " habitus " or official uniform in the King's Colours, white and green, with the name of the Muse Calliope embroidered on it in " silk and gold ". In 1499 when the great Dutch scholar Erasmus visited England for the second time, he was so impressed by Skelton's learning that, in the dedication to Prince Henry of a Latin ode in praise of Britain, he refers to him as " unum Britannicarum litterarum lumen ac docus ", and in an epigram praises him as the combined Homer and Virgil of Britain. In 1498 Skelton entered holy orders and, at an unknown date but probably soon after his ordination, he was appointed rector of Diss in Norfolk. He appears to have retired from Court and gone to live in Diss soon after the turn of the century, and he was certainly there in 1504. Various traditions survived concerning Skelton's life as a parish priest, particularly with regard to his alleged quarrels with his bishop. There seems to be every reason to believe the story that he was secretly married, in defiance of the law which imposed celibacy on the priesthood, and there is good authority for the tradition that he confessed on his death-bed that he regarded the woman with whom he lived as his legal wife. On the other hand, modern research has discovered records which seem to show that he was regarded by the church authorities as a normal and responsible parish priest.

Soon after Henry VIII came to the throne in 1509 he granted to Skelton the title of *Orator Regius*, and the poet now appears to have been again closely associated with the Court. He celebrated the accession to the throne of his old pupil in English and Latin verse, attacked Henry's enemy, King James of Scotland, in a group of poems celebrating the victory of Flodden (1513), and at the king's command engaged in a " flyting " or contest of poetical abuse with Christopher Garnesche, a gentleman usher of the Court. His powerful morality play *Magnificence*, probably written in 1515–16, shows that he regarded himself as no mere rhyming jester but as a serious counsellor of the king and even a critic of his conduct. These years saw the rise of the king's new favourite, Thomas Wolsey : and *Magnificence* reflects Skelton's deep distrust of his policy and his influence on the king.

In 1518 we know Skelton was lodging at Westminster in a house belonging to the Abbot and Convent. Soon after he appears as a bitter and powerful satirist of the abuses of the Church and especially of the conduct and policy of Wolsey. The attacks on Wolsey are veiled in *Colin Clout* (1519–20), but in *Speak Parrot* (1521) he openly condemns the Cardinal's French policy, and in *Why Come Ye Not to Court?* (1522–3) he made a bitter personal onslaught on the king's favourite which is one of the most scathing satires ever addressed to an English statesman. It was probably only the protection of the powerful Howard family that saved him from Wolsey's vengeance. In 1523 he was staying at Sherriff Hutton Castle, the Yorkshire seat of the Howards, where he wrote his long allegorical poem *The Garland of Laurel*. In the same year he composed his last satire on the Scots, an amusing attack on the Scottish Duke of Albany, who had tried to invade England, but was defeated by Thomas Howard, Earl of Surrey, son of Skelton's patron the Duke of Norfolk. This Earl of Surrey was father of Henry Howard, afterwards Earl of Surrey, the famous poet (1517–47), and it is not unlikely that Skelton met him when he was a child of six or seven. *The Garland of Laurel* contains a superb compliment to his mother, the Countess.

Skelton's last important work was an attack on the new Lutheran heretics called *A Replication*, which is directed particularly against the Protestant group at Cambridge headed by Thomas Bilney and Thomas Arthur. Though a bitter critic of the princes of the Church and a castigator of ecclesiastical abuses, Skelton was no Protestant, but, like his contemporary, Sir Thomas More, a faithful son of the Church, who regarded the new heresies with abhorrence. His last years were darkened by the anger of the great Cardinal whom he had attacked with such temerity. According to John Bale, who wrote the earliest account of Skelton (published in 1557), the poet's life was in danger and he only escaped Wolsey's vengeance by taking refuge in the Sanctuary at Westminster, where he presumably still retained the house occupied by him in 1509. He was on excellent terms with John Islip, Abbot of Westminster, and there is no reason to suppose that he suffered any particular hardship by his retirement to the Sanctuary, which at that time covered a considerable area and even included a tavern. He seems to have made a last desperate effort to regain the Cardinal's favour by dedicating to him his two last poems, *The Duke of Albany* and *A Replication*. He died at Westminster on 21 June 1529, and is buried in the chancel of St. Margaret's Church.

His character is full of contradictions and paradoxes. He was at once a ribald wit and a creator of delicate beauty, a rebel and a conservative, a fine classical scholar who derided and mistrusted the New Learning, a faithful son of the Church who defied its laws by his marriage, and who denounced his ecclesiastical superiors in the coarsest and most violent terms.

III

When Skelton began to write, the established mode of serious poetry was the degenerate Chaucerian manner of Lydgate and Hoccleve, heavy-handed craftsmen in verse with a boundless reverence for their master Chaucer, but with none of his fine artistry, his gracious urbanity, or his imaginative vision. In their hands and in those of their successors, Hawes, Barclay, and Bradshaw, the finely balanced metre of Chaucer becomes sprawling doggerel and the dream allegory which he used with such delicate art and literary tact turns into a pedantic convention encouraging intolerable prosiness and prolixity. Their favourite literary device was the use of " aureate diction ", consisting of the liberal use of sonorous polysyllables of Latin origin which are often merely a means of eking out their barrenness of thought. Skelton's earliest poems are written in the prevailing post-Chaucerian manner. These are the elegy on Edward IV and another on the Duke of Northumberland, typical late-medieval laments of a type that was only too prevalent in the fifteenth century, when poets were never tired of repeating the commonplaces that all men are mortal and all flesh is as grass. Yet already in these immature and imitative poems there are touches of humanity and originality that recall Skelton's Scottish contemporaries Henryson and Dunbar rather than the dreary " English Chaucerians ". There is real pathos and dignity in the elegy on Edward

IV, and already some of that directness of speech which is one of Skelton's great gifts, as in the line in which the dead King addresses his queen :

> O Lady Bess, long for me may ye call.

There were other and better traditions of poetry in the fifteenth century besides the aureate post-Chaucerian style. There was the religious tradition growing out of the Latin hymns and carols of the Middle Ages and closely connected with Gothic sculpture and architecture. Skelton's early religious poems belong to this tradition. The best of them, *Woefully Arrayed*, is a kind of Gothic crucifix in verse, an elaborate and finely wrought piece of word-sculpture where the idea of the agony of the Crucified Christ is expressed by means of an intricate pattern of rhyme, assonance, and alliteration that anticipates the experiments of Gerard Manley Hopkins :

> Thus naked am I nailéd, O man, for thy sake !
> I love thee, then love me ; why sleepest thou ? awake !
> Remember my tender heart-root for thee brake,
> With painés my veinés constrainéd to crake.

Another living poetic tradition in the fifteenth century was that of the popular song, closely connected with the art of music, which made notable progress in England after the pioneer work of John Dunstable in the reign of Henry VI. A number of songs are ascribed to Skelton : the finest perhaps is the beautiful lullaby *My Darling Dear*, described by Edith Sitwell as " one of the most drowsy-sounding poems in our language ".

Skelton's first important poem was *The Bowge of Court*. In this remarkable work he actually achieves the miracle of infusing new life into the old dream-allegory in rhyme-royal which was utterly hackneyed and outworn at the end of the fifteenth century. Instead of using the dream convention to typify the situation of the courtly lover or the mourner lamenting a noble friend, he boldly transforms it into a vehicle for a trenchant piece of social criticism on the difficulties and dangers of Court life under the Tudors. The naive *Drede* is a transparent disguise for the poet himself and *Favel*, *Harvy Hafter*, *Riot* and the rest are clearly recognizable as the disreputable sharpers who haunted the fringes of the Court and preyed on simple-minded novices. These rogues are presented with a vividness and humour that was unparalleled in English poetry since Chaucer and Langland :

> He gazed on me with his goatish beard,
> When I looked on him, my purse was half afeared.

Nevertheless in spite of its brilliance and dramatic power *The Bowge of Court* is a pouring of new wine into old bottles ; Skelton's realism and social satire are not really suitable material for the dream-allegory in rhyme-royal. The first poem in which he reveals his full power and originality is *Philip Sparrow*, an elegy on the death of Philip, the pet sparrow of Jane Scrope, a girl at the convent school of Carow near Norwich. Here for the first time he makes full use of the typical Skeltonic metre and style. The metre, short lines of two or three accents rhyming in couplets or triplets, with which he had already experimented in the macabre little poem *Upon a Dead Man's Head*, is, to use the term of G. M. Hopkins, a " sprung rhythm ", akin to the measures of the nursery rhymes; it is probably the descendant of the English four-accent alliterative line, broken into two halves, and combined with the tradition of the short rhyming lines of the Latin " Goliardic " poets of the Middle Ages. It is a splendid instrument for Skelton's swift, colloquial, vivid style, the quality that Mrs. Browning called his " rugged, rapid, picturesque savageness ". Skelton himself has described his own style and metre admirably in *Colin Clout* :

> For though my rhyme be ragged,
> Tatteréd and jaggéd,
> Rudely rain-beaten,
> Rusty and moth-eaten,
> If ye take well therewith,
> It hath in it some pith.

Thomas Churchyard, Skelton's younger contemporary, said of him that " he spoke as he wrote ", and in the work of no English poet do we get a stronger impression of the voice of a living man.

Philip Sparrow was rightly called by S. T. Coleridge an " exquisite and original poem ". A few suggestions from Catullus's poem on Lesbia's sparrow are combined with a parody of the medieval burial service, and on this light, airy framework is set a series of pictures which preserve the charm of Jane and her pet with an almost startling vividness :

> It had a velvet cap,
> And would sit on my lap,
> And seek after small wormés,
> And sometimes white bread-crummés ;
> And many times and oft
> Between my brestés soft
> It woulde lie and rest ;
> It was proper and prest.
>
> Sometime he would gasp
> When he saw a wasp,
> A fly or a gnat,
> He would fly at that ;
> And prettily he would pant
> When he saw an ant.
> Lord, how he would pry
> After the butterfly !
> Lord, how he would hop
> After the gressop !

The Tunning of Elinour Rumming forms a strange contrast with *Philip Sparrow*. Like Swift, with whom he has much in common, Skelton combines an exquisite appreciation of the delicacy and charm of childhood with a terrible vision of the ugliness and foulness of humanity. *The Tunning of Elinour Rumming* is a picture of a low tavern at Leatherhead (Skelton's precise geographical locations are an important element in his poetry). The procession of the hideous old hags who come to drink

Elinour's " noppy ale " is painted with a power and gusto worthy of Skelton's contemporary Jerom Bosch, or of that other great Flemish painter, Pieter Brueghel, who was a child of four when the poet died. The poem is a splendid example of Skelton's precise use of sensuous images. He makes us not only see but touch, smell, and taste some of the horrors of that side of medieval life which is ignored by sentimental Gothic revivalists.

Skelton's flyting poems *Against Garnesche* and his attacks on the Scots are splendid examples of the poetry of abuse, unique perhaps in Southern English, and only rivalled by his exuberant and versatile Scottish contemporary William Dunbar. Here we can see what Mrs. Browning meant when she wrote of Skelton's " wonderful dominion over language " and W. H. Auden when he praised the " Catherine-wheel-like motion " of his verse. His mockery of Garnesche is full of enormous relish in the quality of English words as well as a thorough enjoyment of the fun of parodying the aureate style :

> I say ye solemn Saracen, all black is your ble ;
> As a glede glowing, your eyen glister like glass,
> Rolling in your hollow head, ugly to see ;
> Your teeth tainted with tawny ; your snively snout doth pass,
> Hooked as a hawké's beak, like Sir Topas . . .

Skelton's work as a serious political satirist begins with *Magnificence*. This powerful drama is probably one of the first morality plays to deal with a purely secular subject. The character of Magnificence cannot be precisely equated with that of Henry VIII. He is a symbol of renaissance kingship, misled by false advisers and brought to the verge of ruin by crafty upstart knaves. The analogy with Henry and Wolsey is obvious. The play is an astonishing piece of technical virtuosity in which, as Auden pointed out, the author has succeeded in the difficult task of differentiating his characters by making them speak in different metres.

Colin Clout (1519–20) is the first of Skelton's anti-
clerical satires. The poem is an attack not merely on
Wolsey but on the abuses of the Church in general, and
particularly on the bishops. The figure of the honest
countryman Colin Clout is used to express the rising
popular indignation at ecclesiastical corruptions, which
was the prelude to the Protestant reformation. Here
Skelton is no mere entertainer but for once a prophet,
a voice for an outburst of popular anger and scorn
in early-sixteenth-century London not unlike that
outburst in eighteenth-century Dublin which inspired
Swift's *Drapier's Letters*. The plain man's condemna-
tion of episcopal pride is expressed with a mordant
conciseness and power which raises it above the level of
a merely topical satire :

> What care they though Gil sweat
> Or Jack of the Noke ?
> The poore people they yoke
> With summons and citations
> And excommunications
> About Churches and markét.
> The bishop on his carpét
> At home full soft doth sit.
>
> *   *
>
> Of an abbey ye make a grange;
> Your works they say, are strange;
> So that their founders' souls
> Have lost their beadérolls,
> The money for their masses
> Spent among wanton lasses.

Speak Parrot is the most obscure and involved of Skelton's
poems, an amazing and brilliantly clever arabesque, where
a variety of languages and an enormous range of literary
quotation and allusion are mingled with colloquialisms
and slang in a way that inevitably recalls to the modern
reader the work of such writers as James Joyce, Ezra
Pound, and T. S. Eliot. Here instead of the honest
countryman Colin, the speaker is the learned and fantastic
parrot, obviously Skelton himself, who at the bidding of his

mistress Gallathea pours out a stream of satiric comment on contemporary affairs, especially on the pride and incompetence of Wolsey and on the New Learning in the universities which the Cardinal encouraged. It may seem strange that Skelton, the classical scholar praised by Erasmus, should attack the New Learning, but, as Professor Ian Gordon has shown, Skelton was a humanist of the old school who distrusted the violent innovations of the new academic reformers and feared that the best elements of medieval learning would be lost in the new enthusiasm for Greek studies :

> For *Graece fari* so occupieth the chair
> That *Latinum fari* may fall to rest and sleep
> And *Syllogisari* was drownéd at Stourbridge Fair.

The fiercest of Skelton's attacks on the Cardinal and his most concentrated satire is to be found in *Why Come Ye Not to Court?* Here Skelton overwhelms his adversary with abuse that reminds the reader of the flyting with Garnesche and recalls Mrs. Browning's description of him as " a Silenus drunk with anger ". In *The Garland of Laurel* he returns to the old form of the dream-allegory in rhyme-royal, but he uses it now with a freedom and a colloquial ease comparable with the manner of Byron in *Beppo* and *Don Juan*. Skelton himself is the central figure without any allegorical disguise, and inset in the allegory are the famous little poems in praise of the ladies of the circle of the Countess of Surrey, portraits painted with a tenderness and grace worthy of Skelton's great contemporary Hans Holbein :

> Merry Margaret,
> As midsummer flower,
> Gentle as falcon
> Or hawk of the tower.

Here is a freshness and purity of lyrical utterance which was unsurpassed in English poetry before the Elizabethan age. Skelton's last poem, *A Replication*, is chiefly notable for its impassioned defence of poetry as a ' heavenly inspiration ', where the poet speaks with the voice of a true humanist and anticipates the argument of Sidney's *Defence of Poetry*.

Skelton is not one of the greatest English writers, but he is a poet of real significance, a remarkable artist in language, richly endowed with gifts of direct, incisive speech and lyrical sweetness, in the words of Robert Graves

> Milling an English grist,
> With homely turn and twist.

His work is no mere antiquarian curiosity but a living influence in an age when poets are faced with problems not unlike those of the early sixteenth century and have again sought to use in poetry the rhythms and idioms of common speech.

SELECTIONS FROM SKELTON'S POEMS

I

OF THE DEATH OF THE NOBLE PRINCE EDWARD THE FOURTH

Miseremini mei, ye that be my friendès !   1
   This world hath formed me down to fall :
Now may I endure, when that every thing endès ?
   What creature is born to be eternall ?
Now there is no more but pray for me all :   5
Thus say I Edward, that late was your king,
   And twenty two years ruled this imperiall,
Some unto pleasure, and some to no liking :
   Mercy I ask of my misdoing ;
What availeth, it, friendès, to be my foe,   10
Sith I can not resist, nor amend your complaining ?
   Quia, ecce, nunc in pulvere dormio ?

I sleep now in mould, as it is naturall
   That earth unto earth hath his reverture :
What ordainèd God to be terrestriall,   15
   Without recourse to the earth of nature ?
   Who to live ever may himself assure ?
What is to trust on mutability,
   Sith that in this world nothing may endure,
For now am I gone, that late was in prosperity :   20

---

   1 *Miseremini mei* have pity
on me.
   7 *twenty two* so D. ; M. has
" xxiii ".—Edward reigned from

1461 to 1483 ; *imperiall* empire.
   11 *Sith* since.
   12 *Quia, ecce,* etc. Because,
lo, now I lie in the dust.

To presume thereupon, it is but a vanity,
    Not certain, but as a cherry fair full of woe ;
Reigned not I of late in great felicity ?
    Et ecce nunc in pulvere dormio.

Where was in my life such one as I,   25
    While lady Fortune with me had continuance ?
Granted not she to me to have victory,
    In England to reign, and to contribute France ?
    She took me by the hand and led me a dance,
And with her sugred lips on me she smiled ;   30
    But, what for her dissembled countenance,
I could not beware till I was beguiled,
    Now from this world she hath me exiled,
When I was lothest hence for to go,
And I am in age but, as who saith, a child,   35
Et ecce nunc in pulvere dormio !

                        *   *

I had enough, I held me not content,
    Without remembrance that I should die ;
And more ever to encroach ready was I bent,
    I knew not how long I should it occupy ;   40
    I made the Tower strong, I wist not why ;
I knew not to whom I purchased Tattershall ;
    I amended Dover on the mountain high,
And London I provoked to fortify the wall ;
I made Nottingham a place full royall,   45
    Windsor, Eltham, and many other mo :
Yet at the last I went from them all,
    Et ecce nunc in pulvere dormio !

---

22 *cherry fair* Medieval fairs held in cherry orchards often used a symbol of the fleetingness of life and its pleasures.

28 *contribute* to levy tribute from.

42 *purchased* in the old sense of acquiring, esp. property or land ; *Tattershall* Tattershall Castle, Lincolnshire.

45 *full* M. and L. omit.

46 *Eltham* a palace of the English medieval kings in Kent ; *mo* more.

Where is now my conquest and victory ?
   Where is my riches and my royal array ?   50
Where be my coursers and my horses high ?
   Where is my mirth, my solace, and my play ?
As vanity, to nought all is wandered away.
   O Lady Bess, long for me may ye call !
   For I am departed till doomès day ;   55
But love ye that Lord that is sovereign of all.
Where be my castles and buildings royall ?
   But Windsor alone, now I have no mo.
And of Eton the prayers perpetuall,
   Et ecce, nunc in pulvere dormio !   60

---

54 *Lady Bess*   Elizabeth,   58 *Windsor*   Edward IV was
wife of Edward IV.   buried there.

II

UPON A DEAD MAN'S HEAD

SKELTON LAUREAT

Upon a dead man's head, that was sent to him from an honorable gentlewoman for a token, devised this ghostly meditation in English, convenable in sentence, commendable, lamentable, lacrymable, profitable for the soul.

Your ugly token   5
My mind hath broken
From worldly lust ;
For I have discust
We are but dust,   10
And die we must.
   It is generall
   To be mortall :
I have well espied
No man may him hide   15
From Death hollow-eyed,
With sinews widerèd
And bones shiderèd,
With his worm-eaten maw,
And his gastly jaw   20
Gasping aside,
Naked of hide,
Neither flesh nor fell.
   Then by my councell,
Look that ye spell   25
Well this gospell :
For whereso we dwell

---

4 *lacrymable* tearful.   18 *shiderèd* split, splintered.
17 *widerèd* withered.   23 *fell* skin.

Death doth us quell,
And with us mell.
For all our pampered paunches,   30
There may be no fraunchise,
Nor worldly bliss,
Redeem us from this :
Our days be dated,
To be checkmated   35
With draughtès of death,
Stopping our breath,
Our eyen sinking,
Our bodies stinking,
Our gummès grinning,   40
Our soulès brinning.
To whom, then shall we sue,
For to have rescúe,
But to sweet Jesu,
On us for to rue ?   45
 O goodly child.
Of Mary mild,
Then be our shield !
That we be not exiled
To the dine dale   50
Of bootless bale,
Nor to the lake
Of fiendès black.
But grant us grace
To see thy face,   55
And to purcháse
Thine heavenly place,
And thy paláce,
Full of solace,
Above the sky   60

---

29 *mell* meddle.
31 *fraunchise* enfranchise-
ment, deliverance.
41 *brinning* burning.

50 *dine* dun, dark.
51 *bootless* where there is
no help. M. reads " botemlys ",
i.e. bottomless.

That is so high ;
Eternally
To behold and see
The Trinity !
  Amen.   65
Myrrez vous y.

---

66   *Myrrez vous y*   behold yourself therein.

III

LULLAY

(Extract)

> With, Lullay, lullay, like a child,
> Thou sleepest too long, thou art beguiled.

My darling dear, my daisy flower,   1
   Let me, quod he, lie in your lap.
Lie still, quod she, my paramour,
   Lie still hardily, and take a nap.
His head was heavy, such was his hap,   5
All drowsy dreaming, drowned in sleep,
That of his love he took no keep,
      With, Hey, lullay, lullay, like a child,
      Thou sleepest too long, thou art beguiled.

With ba, ba, ba, and bas, bas, bas   10
   She cherished him both cheek and chin !
That he wist never where he was ;
   He had forgotten all deadly sin.
   He wanted wit her love to win.
He trusted his payment, and lost all his pay   15
She left him sleeping and stale away,
      With Hey, lullay, lullay, like a child,
      Thou sleepest too long, thou art beguiled.

         *   *

2 *quod* quoth.
3 *paramour* sweetheart.
15 *pay* original text reads "pray"; "pay" is D's conjectural emendation.
16 *stale* stole.

IV

WOEFULLY ARRAYED

Woefully arrayed, 1
  My blood, man,
  For thee ran,
It may not be nayed ;
My body blo and wan, 5
  Woefully arrayed.

Behold me, I pray thee, with all thy whole reason,
And be not so hard hearted, and for this encheason,
Sith I for thy soulė sake was slain in good season,
Beguiled and betrayed by Judas' false reason ; 10
  Unkindly entreated,
  With sharp cord sore fretted,
  The Jewės me threated,
They mowėd, they grinnėd, they scornėd me,
Condemnėd to death, as thou mayest see, 15
  Woefully arrayed.

Thus naked am I nailėd, O man, for thy sake !
I love thee, then love me ; why sleepest thou ? awake !
Remember my tender heart-root for thee brake,
With painės my veinės constrainėd to crake ; 20
  Thus tuggėd to and fro,
  Thus wrappėd all in woe,
  Whereas never man was so,
Entreated thus in most cruel wise,
Was like a lamb offered in sacrifice, 25
  Woefully arrayed.

---

4 *nayed* denied.
5 *blo* blue-black, livid.
8 *encheason* cause, reason.
14 *mowėd* made faces at, mocked.
20 *crake* crack.

Of sharp thorn I have worn a crown on my head,
So painèd, so strainèd, so rueful, so red ;
Thus bobbèd, thus robbèd, thus for thy love dead,
Unfeignèd, not dénied my blood for to shed ;　　30
     My feet and handès sore
     The sturdy nailès bore ;
     What might I suffer more
That I have done, O man, for thee ?
Come when thou list, welcome to me,　　35
     Woefully arrayed.

Of recórd thy good Lord I have been and shall be ;
I am thine, thou art mine, my brother, I call thee ;
Thee I love entirely ;　see what is befallen me !
Sore beating, sore threating, to make thee, man, all free ;
     Why art thou unkind ?　　41
     Why hast not mee in mind ?
     Come yet and thou shalt find
Mine endless mercy and grace ;
See how a spear my heart did race,　　45
     Woefully arrayed.

Dear brother, no other thing I of thee desire.
But give me thine heart free to reward mine hire :
I wrought thee, I bought thee from eternal fire :
I pray thee array thee toward my high empire,　　50
     Above the orient,
     Whereof I am regent,
     Lord God omnipotent,
With me to reign in endless wealth ;
Remember, man, thy soulès health.　　55

---

29 *bobbèd* mocked, made a fool of.

35 *list* like.

45 *race* cut or slash.

Woefully arrayed,
My blood, man,
For thee ran.
It may not be nayed ;
My body blo and wan,
    Woefully arrayed.

60

V

THE BOWGE OF COURT

In autumn, when the sun *in Virgine*   1
　　By radiant heat enriped hath our corn ;
When Luna, full of mutability,
　　As emperess the diadem hath worn
　　Of our pole arctic, smiling half in scorn   5
At our folly and our unsteadfastness ;
The time when Mars to warrè him did dress ;

I, calling to mind the great authority
　　Of poets oldè, which full craftily,
Under as covert termès as could be,   10
　　Can touch a truth and cloak it subtilly
　　With freshe utterance full sententiously,
Divers in stylè, some spared not vice to wyte,
Some of morality nobly did endite ;

Whereby I rede their renown and their fame   15
　　May never die, but evermore endure.
I was sore moved to aforce the same,
　　But Ignorance full soon did me discure,
　　And shewed that in this art I was not sure ;
For to illumine, she said, I was too dull,   20
Advising me my pen away to pull,

And not to write : for he so will attain
　　Exceeding further than his conning is,

Title : Bowge French *bouche*, | through which the sun passes in
lit. mouth, i.e. rewards. | early autumn.
　1 *In Virgine* In the sign of | 7 *dress* address.
Virgo, the sign of the Zodiac | 13 *wyte* blame.

25

His head may be hard, but feeble is his brain,
  Yet have I knowen such ere this.   25
  But of reproach surely he may not miss
That climbeth higher than he may footing have :
What and he slide down, who shall him save ?

Thus up and down my mind was drawen and cast,
  That I ne wist what to do was best ;   30
So sore enwearied, that I was at the last
  Enforced to sleep and for to take some rest,
  And to lie down as soon as I me dressed.
At Harwich port slumbering as I lay
In mines hostès house, called Powers Key.   35

Methought I saw a ship, goodly of sail,
  Come sailing forth into the haven broad,
Her tackling rich and of high appareil :
  She cast an anchor, and there she lay at road.
  Merchants her boarded to see what she had load : 40
Therein they found royal merchandise.
Freighted with pleasure of what ye could devise.

But then I thought I would not dwell behind ;
  Among all other I put myself in press.
Then there could I none acquaintance find :   45
  There was much noise ; anon one cried, ' Cease ! '
  Sharply commanding each man hold his peace.
' Masters,' he said, ' the ship that ye here see
The Bowge of Court is hight for certainty.

' The owner thereof is lady of estate   50
  Whose name to tell is dame Sauncepere ;

---

28 *and* if.
33 *dressed* not in the modern
sense ; here = addressed, applied,
myself.

35 *Powers Key* an inn at
Harwich.
51 *Sauncepere* incomparable.

Her merchandise is rich and fortunate,
　　But who will have it must pay therefor dear ;
　　This royal chaffer that is shipped here
Is called Favor, to stand in her good grace.'   55
Then should ye see there pressing in apace.

Of one and other that would this lady see :
　　Which sat behind a travès of silke fine,
Of gold of tissue the finest that might be,
　　In a throne which far clearer did shine   60
　　Than Phoebus in his sphere celestine ;
Whose beauty, honour, goodly port
I have too little conning to report.

But of each thing there as I took heed,
　　Among all other was written in her throne   65
In gold letters, these words, which I did read :
　　Gardez le fortune, qui est mavelz et bone !
　　And, as I stood reading this verse myself alone,
Her chief gentlewoman, Danger by her name,
Gave me a taunt, and said I was to blame.   70

To be so pert to press so proudly up :
　　She said she trowed that I had eaten sauce ;
She asked if ever I drank of sauce's cup.
　　And I then softly answered to that clause.
　　That so to say I had given her no cause.   75
Then asked she me, ' Sir, so God thee speed,
What is thy name ? ' and I said, it was Drede.

---

58 *travès* a low screen, cur-
tain.
61 *celestine* celestial.
67 *Gardez le fortune*, etc.
Beware of Fortune, which is evil
and good.

69 *Danger* disdain (personi-
fied). Danger, a male character,
is the guardian of the rose
(i.e. beauty) in *Le Roman de la
Rose*.
72 *trowed* believed.

' What moved thee,' quod she, ' hither to come ? '
   ' Forsooth,' quod I, ' to buy some of your ware.'
And with that word on me she gave a glome   80
   With browės bent, and 'gan on me to stare
   Full dainously, and fro me she did fare,
Leaving me standing as a mazėd man,
To whom there came another gentlewoman.

Desire her name was, and so she me told,   85
   Saying to me, ' Brother, be of good cheer,
Abash you not, but hardėly be bold,
   Advance yourself to approach and come near :
   What though our chaffer be never so dear,
Yet I advise you to speak, for any drede :   90
Who spareth to speak, in faith, he spareth to speed.'

' Mistress,' quod I, ' I have none acquaintance
   That will for me be mediator and mean ;
And this another, I have but small substance.'
' Peace,' quod Desire, ' ye speak not worth a bean !   95
   If ye have not, in faith, I will you lene
A precious jewel, no richer in this land :
Bone aventure have here now in your hand.

' Shift now therewith, let see, as ye can
   In Bowge of Court chevisaunce to make ;   100
For I dare say that there nis earthly man
   But, an he can *bone aventure* take,
   There can no favour nor friendship him foresake ;
Bone aventure may bring you in such case
That ye shall stand in favour and in grace.   105

' But of one thing I warn you ere I go :
   She that steereth the ship, make her your friend.'

---

80 *glome* glum look.
89 *chaffer* merchandise.
96 *lene* lend.

98 *Bone aventure* good fortune.
100 *chevisaunce* profit, gain.

' Mistress,' quod I, ' I pray you tell me why so,
  And how I may that way and meanės find.'
    ' Forsooth,' quod she, ' however blow the wind,   110
Fortune guideth and ruleth all our ship :
Whom she hateth shall over the sea board skip ;

' Whom she loveth, of all pleasure is rich,
  While she laugheth and hath lust for to play ;
Whom she hateth, she casteth in the ditch,   115
  For when she frowneth, she thinketh to make a fray ;
  She cherisheth him, and him she casteth away.'
' Alas,' quod I, ' how might I have her sure ? '
' In faith,' quod she, ' by *bone aventure.*'

Thus, in a row, of merchants a great rout   120
  Sued to Fortune that she would be their friend :
They throng in fast, and flocked her about ;
  And I with them prayed her to have in mind,
  She promised to us all she would be kind :
Of Bowge of Court she asketh what we would have,   125
And we asked Favour, and Favour she us gave.

DREDE

The sail is up, Fortune ruleth our helm,
  We want no wind to pass now over all ;
Favour we have tougher than any elm,
  That will abide and never from us fall :   130
  But under honey offtime lieth bitter gall :
For, as methought, in our ship I did see
Full subtil persons, in number four and three.

The first was Favell, full of flattery,
  With fables false that well could feign a tale ;   135

---

112 *sea board* M. has " shyp borde ".

134 *Favell* " the fallow horse proverbial as the type of fraud, cunning or duplicity . . . hence used as a mere personification of cunning or duplicity " (*N.E.D.*). The exact colour denoted by " fallow " is unknown.

The second was Suspect, which that daily
   Misdeemed each man, with face deadly and pale ;
   And Harvy Hafter, that well could pick a male,
With other four of their affinity,
Disdain, Riot, Dissimuler, Subtility.   140

Fortune their friend, with whom oft she did dance ;
   They could not fail, they thought, they were so sure ;
And oftentimes I would myself advance
   With them to make solace and pleasúre ;
   But my disport they could not well endure :   145
They said they hated for to deal with Drede.
Then Favell 'gan with fair speech me to feed.

FAVELL

' No thing earthly that I wonder so sore
   As of your conning, that is so excellent ;
Dainty to have with us such one in store,   150
   So virtuously that hath his dayes spent ;
   Fortune to you giftés of grace hath lent :
Lo, what it is a man to have conning !
All earthly treasure it is surmounting.

' Ye be an apt man, as any can be found,   155
   To dwell with us, and serve my lady's grace ;
Ye be to her, yea, worth a thousand pound !
   I heard her speak of you within short space,
   When there were divers that sore did you menáce ;
And, though I say it, I was myself your friend,   160
For here be divers to you that be unkind.

' But this one thing—ye may be sure of me ;
   For, by that Lord that bought dear all mankind,

---

138 *Harvey Hafter* " haft "   Dodger ; *male* bag, wallet.
is an old word meaning to trick
or dodge. Harvey Hafter = Artful   153 *conning* learning.

I cannot flatter, I must be plain to thee ;
   And ye need ought, man, shew to me your mind,   165
   For ye have me whom faithful ye shall find ;
Whiles I have ought, by God, thou shalt not lack,
And if need be, a bold word I dare crack !

' Nay, nay, be sure, whiles I am on your side
   Ye may not fall, trust me, ye may not fail.   170
Ye stand in favour, and Fortune is your guide,
   And, as she will, so shall our great ship sail :
   These lewd cockwats shall nevermore prevail
Against you hardėly, therefore be not afraid ;
Farewell till soon ; but no word that I said.   175

DREDE

Then thankėd I him for his great gentleness :
   But, as methought, he ware on him a cloak
That lined was with doubtful doubleness ;
   Methought, of words that he had full a poke ;
   His stomach stuffed oft times did reboke.   180
Suspect, methought, met him at a braid,
And I drew near to hark what they two said.

' In faith,' quod Suspect, ' spake Drede no word of me ? '
   ' Why ? what then ? wilt thou let me to speak ?
He saith, he cannot well accord with thee.'   185
   ' Twist,' quod Suspect, ' go play ! him I ne reke ! '
   ' By Christ,' quod Favell, ' Drede is sullen freke.
What, let us hold him up, man, for a while ? '
' Yea so,' quod Suspect, ' he may us both beguile.'

---

173   *cockwats* M. reads cok-
witts ; conceited fellows.
  179 *poke* bag.
  180 *reboke* belch.

181 *at a braid* in a twinkling
of an eye.
186 *reke* pay heed to.
187 *freke* fellow.

And when he came walking soberly,   190
    With hum and ha, and with a crooked look,
Methought, his head was full of jealousy,
    His eyen rolling, his handės fast they quoke ;
    And to meward the straitė way he took.
' God speed, brother ! ' to me quod he then ;   195
And thus to talk with me he began.

SUSPECT

' Ye remember the gentleman right now
    That communed with you, methought a party space ?
Beware of him, for, I make God avow,
    He will beguile you and speak fair to your face.   200
    Ye never dwelt in such another place,
For here is none that dare well other trust—
But I would tell you a thing, an I durst !

' Spake he, i' faith, no word to you of me ?
    I wot, an he did, ye would me tell.   205
I have a favour to you, whereof it be
    That I must shew you much of my counsél.
    But I wonder what the devil of hell
He said of me, when he with you did talk !
By mine advice use not with him to walk.   210

' The sovranest thing that any man may have
    Is little to say, and much to hear and see ;
For, but I trusted you, so God me save,
    I would nothing so plain be :
    To you only, methink, I durst shrive me,   215
For now am I plenarly disposėd
To shew you things that may not be disclosėd.'

---

215 *shrive* confess.   216 *plenarly* fully.

DREDE

Then I assured him my fidelity
   His counsel secret never to discure,
If he could find in heart to trustê me ;   220
   Else I prayed him, with all my busy cure,
   To keep it himself, for then he might be sure.
That no man earthly could him bewray,
Whiles of his mind it were locked with the key.

' By God,' quod he, ' this and thus it is ' ;   225
   And of his mind he shewed me all and some
' Farewell,' quod he, ' we will talk more of this ' :
   So he departed where he would be come.
   I dare not speak, I promised to be dumb.
But, as I stood musing in my mindê.   230
Harvy Hafter came leaping, light as lindê.

Upon his breast he bare a versing-box,
   His throat was clear, and lustily could fayne.
Methought his gown was all furred with fox,
   And ever he sang, ' Sith I am nothing plain.'   235
   To keep him from picking it was a great pain :
He gazed on me with his goatish beard,
When I looked on him, my purse was half afeard.

HARVY HAFTER

' Sir, God you save ! why look ye so sad ?
   What thing is that I may do for you ?   240
A wonder thing that ye wax not mad !
   For, an I study should as ye do now,
   My wit would waste, I make God a vow !
Tell me your mind : methink ye make a verse ;
I could it scan, an ye would it rehearse !   245

---

219 *discure* disclose.   232 *versing-box* probably a
223 *bewray* betray.   dice-box.
231 *lindê* linden tree.

' But to the point shortly to proceed,
   Where hath your dwelling been ere ye came here ?
For, as I trow, I have seen you indeed
   Ere this, when that ye made me royal cheer.
   Hold up the helm, look up, and let God steer :   250
I would be merry, what wind that ever blow !
Heave and ho rumbelow, row the boat, Norman, row !

' Princes of Youth ' can ye sing by rote ?
   Or ' Shall I sail with you ' a fellowship assay ?
For on the book I cannot sing a note.   255
   Would to God, it would please you some day
   A ballad book before me for to lay,
And learn me to sing re mi fa sol !
And, when I fail, bob me on the noll.

' Lo, what is to you a pleasure great   260
   To have that conning and ways that ye have !
By Goddès soul, I wonder how ye get
   So great pleasure, or who to you it gave.
   Sir, pardon me, I am an homely knave,
To be with you thus pert and thus bold :   265
But ye be welcome to our household.

' And, I dare say, there is no man therein
   But would be glad of your company.
I wist never man that so soon could win
   The favour that ye have with my lady.   270
   I pray to God that it may never die.
It is your fortune for to have that grace—
As I be saved, it is a wonder case !

---

252 *Heave and ho,* etc. title
of popular song.

253 *Princes of Youth* title
of popular song.

254 *Shall I sail with you*
title of popular song.

259 *bob me on the noll* knock
me on the head.

' For, as for me, I served here many a day
   And yet unneth I can have my living :   275
But, I require you, no worde that I say !
   For, an I know any earthly thing
   That is again you, ye shall have weeting :
And ye be welcome, sir, so God me save !
I hope hereafter a friend of you to have.'   280

DREDE

With that, as he departed so from me,
   Anon there met with him, as methought,
A man, but wonderly beseen was he ;
   He looked hawtie, he set each man at nought ;
   His gawdy garment with scornès was all wrought ;   285
With indignation lined was his hood :
   He frowned, as he would swear by Cockes blood.

He bote the lip, he looked passing coy ;
   His face was belimmed, as bees had him stung :
It was no time with him to jape nor toy.   290
   Envy had wasted his liver and his lung,
   Hatred by the heart so had him wrung
That he looked pale as ashes to my sight.
Disdain, I ween, this comerous crab is hight.

To Harvy Hafter then he spake of me,   295
   And I drew near to hark what they two said.
' Now,' quod Disdain, ' as I shall savèd be,
   I have great scorn, and am right evil apayed.'
   Then quod Harvy ' Why art thou so dismayed ? '
' By Christ,' quod he, ' for it is shame to say :   300
To see Johan Dawes that came but yesterday.

---

284 *hawtie* haughty.
288 *bote* bit.
289 *belimmed* disfigured.
294 M. reads " his come-

rous crabes hyghte ", *comerous*
troublesome.
301 *Johan Dawes* name for a
foolish fellow (i.e. Drede).

' How he is now taken in conceit,
   This Doctor Dawcock, Drede, I ween, he hight.
By Goddès bones, but if we have some sleight
   It is like he will stande in our light.'   305
     ' By God,' quod Harvy, ' and it so happen might.
Let us therefore shortly at a word
Find some means to cast him overboard.'

' By him that me bought,' then quod Disdain,
   ' I wonder sore he is in such conceit ! '   310
' Turd ! ' quod Hafter, ' I will thee nothing feign,
   There must for him be laid some pretty bait ;
   We twain, I trow, be not without deceit :
First pick a quarrel, and fall out with him then,
And so outface him with a card of ten.'   315

Forthwith he made on me a proud assault,
   With scornful look moved all in mood ;
He went about to take me in a fault ;
   He frowned, he stared, he stampèd where he stood.
   I looked on him, I wend he had been wood.   320
He set the arm proudly under the side,
And in this wise he 'gan with me to chide.

DISDAIN

' Rememberest thou what thou said yesternight ?
   Wilt thou abide by the words again ?
By God, I have of thee now great despite !   325
   I shall thee anger once in every vein :
   It is great scorn to see such an haine

---

303 *Doctor Dawcock* much the same as " Johan Dawes ".

311 M. reads " sayne " probably a mistake for " fayne ".

315 *outface him with a card of ten* an expression apparently derived from a card game (possibly primero), meaning " to bully, to attack by impudence of face ".—D.

317 *in mood* angrily.

320 *wood* mad.

327 *haine* rascal.

As thou art, one that came but yesterday,
With us old servants suche masters to play !

' I tell thee, I am of countenance :   330
   What weenest I were ? I trow thou know not me !
By Goddes wounds, but for displeasance,
   Of my quarrel soon would I venged be.
   But no force, I shall once meet with thee.
Come when it will, oppose thee I shall,   335
Whatsomever adventure thereof fall.

' Trowest thou, drevil, I say, thou gawdy knave,
   That I have deinte to see thee cherished thus ?
By Goddes side, my sword thy beard shall shave !
   Well, once thou shalt be charmed, ywis.   340
   Nay, straw for tales, thou shalt not rule us :
We be thy betters, and so thou shalt us take,
Or we shall thee out of thy clothes shake ! '

DREDE

With that came Riot, rushing all at once,
   A rusty gallant, to-ragged and to-rent ;   345
And on the board he whirled a pair of bones,
' *Quater trey dews* ' he clattered as he went.
' Now have at all, by Saint Thomas of Kent ! '
And ever he threw and cast I wote n'ere what :
His hair was growen thorough out his hat.   350

Then I beheld how he disguised was :
   His head was heavy for watching over night,
His eyen bleered, his face shone like a glass ;
   His gown so short that it ne cover might
   His rump, he went so all for summer light.   355

---

337 *drevil* base fellow.
341 *straw* i.e. a straw
347 *Quater trey dews* four, three, two (dicing terms).

348 *Saint Thomas of Kent* St. Thomas a Becket.
351 *disguised* altered in appearance.

His hose was garded with a list of green,
Yet at the knee they were broken, I ween.

His coat was checked with patches red and blue ;
  Of Kirby Kendal was his short demy ;
And aye he sang, ' In faith, deacon, thou crew ' ;   360
  His elbow bare, he ware his gear so nigh ;
  His nose a-dropping, his lippes were full dry ;
And by his side his whinyard and his pouch,
The devil might dance therein for any crowch.

*   *

What should I tell more of his ribaldry ?   365
  I was ashamèd so to hear him prate :
He had no pleasure but in harlotry.
  ' Ay,' quod he, ' in the devil's date,
  What art thou ? I saw thee now but late.'
' Forsooth,' quod I, ' in this court I dwell now.'   370
' Welcome,' quod Riot, ' I make God avow.'

RIOT

' And, sir, in faith why com'st not us among
  To make thee merry, as other fellows done ?
Thou must swear and stare, man, all day long,
  And wake all night, and sleep till it be noon ;   375
  Thou mayest not study, or muse on the moon ;
This world is nothing but eat, drink, and sleep,
And thus with us good company to keep.

' Pluck up thine heart upon a merry pin,
  And let us laugh a pluck or twain at nale :   380

---

356 *garded* ornamented ; *list* border.

359 *Kirby Kendal* green cloth made at Kendal in Westmoreland ; *demy* tune.

360 *In faith*, etc. first line of a song

363 *whinyard* sword.

364 *crowch* cross, i.e. small coin. A stanza is omitted here.

380 *pluck* a snatch, a bout, a " go " ; *at nale* at an alehouse.

What the devil, man, mirth is here within !
  What, lo man, see here of dice a bale !
  A bridling-cast for that is in thy male !
Now have at all that lieth upon the board !
Fie on these dice, they be not worth a turd !   385

' Have at the hazard, or at the dozen brown,
  Or else I pass a penny to a pound !
Now, would to God, thou would lay money down !
  Lord, how that I woulde cast it full round !
  Ay, in my pouch a buckle I have found,   390
The arms of Calais, I have no coin nor cross !
I am not happy, I run aye on the loss.'

                    *   *

                    DREDE

Gone is this knave, this ribald foul and lewd.
  He ran as fast as ever that he might.
Unthriftiness in him may well be shewed,   395
  For whom Tyburn groaneth both day and night.
  And, as I stood and cast aside my sight,
Disdain I saw with Dissimulation
Standing in sad communication.

But there was pointing and nodding with the head,   400
  And many wordes said in secret wise ;
They wandered aye, and stood still in no stead :
  Methought always Dissimuler did devise.
  Me passing sore mine heart then 'gan agrise,
I deemed and dread their talking was not good.   405
Anon Dissimuler came where I stood.

---

383 *bridling-cast* probably a
cup of wine, a " stirrup cup ".
  382 *bale* a " bale of dice "
was a set of dice for any special
game " (*N.E.D.*).
  392 Two stanzas are omitted.

396 *Tyburn* i.e. the gallows.
  404 *agrise* all old eds. read
" aryse " ; " agryse " is D.'s
emendation. It means " to
cause to shudder ".
  405 *dread* dreaded.

Then in his hood I saw there faces twain :
　That one was lean and like a pinèd ghost,
That other looked as he would me have slain ;
　And to meward as he 'gan for to coast,   410
　When that he was even at me almost,
I saw a knife hid in his one sleeve,
Whereon was written this word, *Mischief*.

And in his other sleeve, methought, I saw
　A spoon of gold, fully of honey sweet,   415
To feed a fool, and for to prove a daw ;
　And on that sleeve these wordes were writ,
　A false abstract cometh from a false concrete.
His hood was side, his cope was russet gray :
These were the words that he to me did say.   420

DISSIMULATION

' How do ye, master ? ye look so soberly !
　As I be saved at the dreadful day,
It is a perilous vice, this envý.
　Alas, a conning man ne dwelle may
　In no place well, but foolès with him fray.   425
But as for that, conning hath no foe
Save him that nought can, Scripture saith so.

' I know your virtue and your literature
　By that little conning that I have :
Ye be maligned sore, I you ensure ;   430
　But ye have craft yourself alway to save.
　It is great scorn to see a misproud knave
With a clerke than conning is to prate :
Let them go louse them, in the devil's date !

419　*side* hanging down, long.　sense of the Italian virtù=power,
428　*virtue* probably in the　accomplishment.

' For albeit that this 'long not to me,   435
   Yet on my back I bear such lewd dealing :
Right now I spake with one, I trow, I see ;
   But what a straw !   I may not tell all thing !
   By God, I say there is great heart-burning
Between the person ye wot of and you.   440
Alas, I could not deal so with a Jew !

' I would each man were as plain as I !
   It is a world, I say, to hear of some :
I hate this feigning, fie upon it, fie !
   A man cannot wot where to be come.   445
I wis I could tell—but humlery, hum !
I dare not speak, we be so laid await,
For all our courte is full of deceit.

' Now by Saint Francis, that holy man and friar,
   I hate these ways again you that they take !   450
Were I as you, I woulde ride them full near.
   And, by my troth, but if an end they make,
   Yet will I say some wordès for your sake
That shall them anger, I hold thereon a groat :
For some shall, ween, be hanged by the throat !   455

' I have a stopping oyster in my poke,
   Trust me, an if it come to a need !
But I am loath for to raise a smoke,
   If ye could be otherwise agreed.
   And so I would it were, so God me speed,   460
For this may breed to a confusion
Without God make a good conclusion.

' Nay, see where yonder standeth teder man !
   A flattering knave and false he is, God wot ;

---

435   *'long*   belong.

449   *Saint Francis*   St. Francis of Assisi (1181–1226), founder of the Order of Franciscan Friars.

455   *ween* for " I ween ".

456   *stopping oyster* something to stop your mouth with.

463   *teder* t'other.

The drevil standeth to harken, and he can.   465
   It were more thrift he bought him a newe coat ;
   It will not be, his purse is not on float :
All that he weareth, it is borrowed ware,
His wit is thin, his hood is threadebare.

' More could I say, but what this is enow :   470
   Adew till soon, we shall speak more of this.
Ye must be ruled as I shall tell you how ;
   Amends may be of that is now amiss.
   And I am yours, sir, so have I bliss,
In every point that I can do or say.   475
Give me your hand, farewell, and have good-day ! '

DREDE

Suddenly, as he departed me fro,
   Came pressing in one in a wonder array.
Ere I was ware, behind me he said, Bo !
   Then I, astonied of that sudden fray,   480
   Start all at once, I liked nothing his play :
For, if I had not quickly fled the touch,
He had plucked out the nobles of my pouch.

He was trussed in a garment strait :
   I have not seen such another page ;   485
For he could well upon a casket wait ;
   His hood all pounsed and garded like a cage ;
   Light lime-finger ! he took none other wage.
' Hearken,' quod he, ' lo here mine hand in thine !
To us welcome thou art, by Saint Quintine.'   490

---

483 *nobles* coins worth six shillings and eightpence.

486 *upon a casket* perhaps a reference to some duty of a nobleman's page.

487 *pounsed* ornamented with figures or letters ; *garded* provided with a " guard " or ornamental border.

490 *Saint Quintine* St. Quintin, a Roman said to have preached Christianity in Gaul and to have been martyred in Picardy in A.D. 287.

DECEIT

' But, by that Lord that is one, two, and three,
   I have an errand to round in your ear . . .
He told me so, by God, ye may trust me,
   Parde, remember when ye were there,
There I winked on you—wot ye not where ?   495
In A loco, I mean juxta B :
Who is him that is blind and may not see !

' But to hear the subtilty and the craft,
   As I shall tell you, if ye will hark again !
And, when I saw the whoreson would you haft,   500
   To hold mine hand, by God, I had great pain :
   For forthwith there I had him slain,
But that I drede murder would come out :
Who dealeth with shrews hath need to look about ! '

DREDE

And as he rounded thus in mine ear   505
   Of false collusion confettered by assent,
Methought I see lewd fellows here and there
   Come for to slay me of mortal intent.
   And, as they came, the shipboard fast I hent,
And thought to leap, and even with that woke,   510
Caught pen and ink, and wrote this little book.

I would therewith no man were miscontent,
   Beseeching you that shall it see or read
In every point to be indifferent,
   Sith all in substance of slumbering doth proceed.   515
   I will not say it is matter indeed,
But yet oft-time such dreamès be found true.
Now construe ye what is the residue !

---

500   *haft*   see above, l. 138 n.

VI

PHILIP SPARROW

(Extract)

Pla ce bo !   1
Who is there, who ?
Di le xi !
Dame Margery.
Fa, re, my, my.   5
Wherefore and why, why ?
For the soul of Philip Sparrow,
That was late slain at Carow,
Among the Nonès Black.
For that sweet soulès sake,   10
And for all sparrowès' souls
Set in our bede-rolls,
Pater noster qui,
With an *Ave Mari,*
And with the corner of a Creed,   15
The more shall be your meed.

When I remember again
How my Philip was slain,
Never half the pain
Was between you twain,   20

---

1 *Pla ce bo* the first words
of the Roman Office for the Dead:
Placebo Domino : " I will please
the Lord ".

3 The first words of Ps. cxvi:
" I love the Lord because he hath
heard ".

8 *Carow* a convent in the
suburbs of Norwich where
Joanna was being educated.
9 *Nonès Black* Benedictine
nuns.
12 *bede-rolls* list of persons
to be prayed for.
13 *Pater noster* beginning
of the Latin version of the Lord's
Prayer.

Pyramus and Thisbe,
As then befell to me.
I wept and I wailed,
The tears down hailed,
But nothing it availed   25
To call Philip again,
Whom Gib, our cat, hath slain.

    Gib, I say, our cat
Worrowèd her on that
Which I loved best.   30
It cannot be exprest
My sorrowful heaviness,
But all without redress !
For within that stound,
Half slumbering, in a sound   35
I fell downe to the ground.

    Unneth I cast mine eyes
Toward the cloudy skies.
But when I did behold
My sparrow dead and cold,   40
No creature but that wold
Have ruèd upon me,
To behold and see
What heaviness did me pang :
Wherewith my hands I wrang,   45
That my sinews crackèd,
As though I had been rackèd,
So pained and so strainèd
That no life wellnigh remainèd.

    I sighed and I sobbèd,   50
For that I was robbèd

---

21 *Pyramus and Thisbe* fa-   29 *worrowèd* worried.
mous Babylonian lovers described   34 *stound* hour.
by Ovid ; see *A Midsummer*   37 *unneth* scarcely.
Night's Dream.   42 *ruèd* taken pity.

Of my sparrowès life.
O maiden, widow, and wife,
Of what estate ye be,
Of high or low degree,   55
Great sorrow then ye might see,
And learn to weep at me !
Such painès did me freat
That mine heart did beat,
My visage pale and dead,   60
Wan, and blue as lead :
The pangs of hateful death
Wellnigh had stopped my breath.

   Heu, heu, me,
That I am woe for thee !   65
Ad Dominum, cum tribularer, clamavi.
Of God nothing else crave I
But Philip's soul to keep
From the marees deep
Of Acherontès well,   70
That is a flood of hell ;
And from the great Pluto,
The prince of endless woe ;
And from foul Alecto,
With visage black and blo ;   75
And from Medusa, that mare,
That like a fiend doth stare ;
And from Megaera's adders
For ruffling of Philip's feathers,
And from her fiery sparklíngs   80
For burning of his wings ;

---

58 *freat* fret, torture.

64 *Heu, heu, me* Alas, alas
for me.

66 *Ad Dominum*, etc. Ps. cxx.
1. : " In my distress I cried unto
the Lord ".

69 *marees* marsh.

74–78 *Alecto, Medusa, Megaera* Alecto and Megaera were
two of the Furies of Greek
legend ; Medusa was one of the
Gorgons.

75 *blo* see above, p. 22, n.

And from the smokès sour
Of Proserpina's bower;
And from the dennès dark
Where Cerberus doth bark,   85
Whom Theseus did affray,
Whom Hercules did outray,
As famous Poetès say ;
From that hell-hound
That lieth in chaines bound,   90
With ghastly headès three ;
To Jupiter pray we
That Philip preserved may be !
Amen, say ye with me,
    Do mi nus,   95
Help now, sweet Jesus !
Levavi oculos meos in montes.

Would God I had Zenophontes,
Or Socrates the wise,
To shew me their device   100
Moderately to take
This sorrow that I make
For Philip Sparrow's sake !
So fervently I shake,
I feel my body quake ;   105
So urgently I am brought
Into careful thought.
Like Andromach, Hector's wife,
Was weary of her life,
When she had lost her joy,   110
Noble Hector of Troy ;
In like manner also
Increaseth my deadly woe,
For my sparrow is go.

---

84 *dennès* dens.
87 *outray* vanquish.
97 Ps. cxxi. 1 : " I will lift
up mine eyes unto the hills ".
  98 *Zenophontes* probably
Xenophon.

It was so pretty a fool,   115
It would sit on a stool,
And learned after my school
For to keep his cut,
With ' Philip, keep your cut ! '

It had a velvet cap,   120
And would sit upon my lap,
And seek after small wormès,
And sometime white bread-crummès ;
And many times and oft
Between my brestès soft   125
It would lie and rest ;
It was proper and prest.

Sometime he would gasp
When he saw a wasp ;
A fly or a gnat,   130
He would fly at that ;
And prettily he would pant
When he saw an ant,
Lord, how he would pry
After the butterfly !   135
Lord, how he would hop
After the gressop !
And when I said, ' Phip, Phip ! '
Then he would leap and skip,
And take me by the lip.   140
Alas, it will me slo
That Philip is gone me fro !

Si in i qui ta tes . . .
Alas, I was evil at ease !

---

118 *keep his cut* behave him-self well.
127 *prest* alert, sprightly.
137 *gressop* grass-hopper.
143 Ps. cxxx. 3 : " If thou, Lord, shouldest mark iniquities ".

De pro fun dis cla ma vi,   145
When I saw my sparrow die !

   Now, after my doom
Dame Sulpicia at Rome,
Whose name registered was
For ever in tables of brass,   150
Because that she did pass
In poesy to indite
And eloquently to write,
Thou she would pretend,
My sparrow to commend,   155
I trow she could not amend
Reporting the virtues all
Of my sparrow royall.

   For it would come and go,
And fly so to and fro ;   160
And on me it would leap
When I was asleep,
And his fathers shake,
Wherewith he woulde make
Me often for to wake,   165
And for to take him in
Upon my naked skin.
God wot, we thought no sin ;
What though he crept so low ?
It was no hurt, I trow   170
He did nothing, perdè,
But sit upon my knee.
Philip, though he were nice,

---

145 Ps. cxxx. 1 : "Out of the depths have I cried unto thee".
147 *doom* judgment.
148 *Sulpicia* the name of two Roman poetesses, one of whom lived in the reign of Augustus and the other in that of Domitian.

J.S.—4

In him it was no vice.
Philip had leave to go   175
To peck my little toe ;
Philip might be bold
And do what he wold :
Philip would seek and take
All the fleas black   180
That he could there espy
With his wanton eye.

   O pe ra,
La, sol, fa, fa,
Confitebor tibi, Domine, in toto cor de meo ! 185
Alas, I would ride and go
A thousand mile of ground !
If any such might be found
It were worth an hundred pound
Of King Croesus' gold,   190
Or of Attalus the old,
The riche prince of Pergame,
Whoso list the story to see.
Cadmus, that his sister sought,
An he should be bought   195
For gold and fee,
He should over the sea
To wete if he could bring
Any of the offspring,
Or any of the blood.   200
But whoso understood.
Of Medea's art,
I would I had a part
Of her crafty magic !
My sparrow then should be quick   205

183–5 Ps. ix. 1 : " I will praise thee, O Lord, with my whole heart ".

192 *Pergame* Pergamus, an ancient kingdom in Asia Minor.
198 *wete* find out.

With a charm or twain,
And play with me again.
But all this is in vain
Thus for to complain.

    I took my sampler once   210
Of purpose, for the nonce,
To sew with stitches of silk
My sparrow white as milk,
That by representation
Of his image and fashion   215
To me it might import
Some pleasure and comfort,
For my solace and sport.
But when I was sewing his beak,
Methought my sparrow did speak,   220
And opened his pretty bill,
Saying, ' Maid, ye are in will
Again me for to kill,
Ye prick me in the head ! '
With that my needle waxèd red,   225
Methought, of Philip's blood ;
Mine hair right upstood,
I was in such a fray
My speech was taken away.
I cast down that there was,   230
And said, ' Alas, alas,
How cometh this to pass ? '
My fingers, dead and cold,
Could not my sampler hold :
My needle and thread   235
I threw away for dread.
The best now that I may
Is for his soul to pray :
A porta inferi

---

239 *A porta inferi* quotation from the Roman Office for
the Dead : " From the gate of
hell, O Lord, save his spirit".

Good Lord, have mercy   240
Upon my sparrow's soul,
Written in my bede-roll !

  Au di vi vo cem,
Japhet, Cam, and Shem,
Ma, gni fi cat,   245
Shew me the right path
To the hills of Armony,
Whereon the birds yet cry,
Of your father's boat,
That was sometime afloat,   250
And now they lie and rot ;
Let some poetès write
Deucalion's flood it hight.
But as verily as ye be
The natural sonnes three   255
Of Noè the patriarch,
That made that great ark,
Wherein he had apes and owls,
Beasts, birds, and fowls,
That if ye can find   260
Any of my sparrow's kind
(God send the soul good rest !)
I would have yet a nest
As pretty and as prest
As my sparrow was.   265
But my sparrow did pass
All sparrows of the wood
That were since Noè's flood,

243–5 *Audivi vocem* antiphon in the Roman Office for the
Dead : " I heard a voice (from
heaven) . . ." (Rev. xiv. 13).
   244 *Japhet, Cam, and Shem*
names of the sons of Noah (Noe)
in the Vulgate.
   245 *Magnificat* first word of

the Canticle of the Virgin (Luke i.
46), in the Vulgate used in the
Office for the Dead : " My soul
doth magnify (the Lord) ".
   247 *Armony*   Armenia.
Mount Ararat, on which the ark
rested after the Flood, was situ-
ated there.

Was never none so good.
King Philip of Macedony   270
Had no such Philip as I,
No, no, sir, hardély !

    That vengeance I ask and cry,
By way of exclamation,
On all the whole nation   275
Of Cattés wild and tame :
God send them sorrow and shame !
That Cat specially
That slew cruelly
My little pretty sparrow   280
That I brought up at Carow.

    O cat of carlish kind,
The fiend was in thy mind
When thou my bird untwined !
I would thou hadst been blind !   285
The leopardés savdge,
The lions in their rage
Might catch thee in their paws,
And gnaw thee in their jaws !
The serpents of Libany   290
Might sting thee venomously !
The dragons with their tongues
Might poison thy liver and lungs !
The manticors of the mountáins
Might feed them on thy brains !   295

    Melanchates, that hound
That plucked Actaeon to the ground,
Gave him his mortal wound,

---

282 *carlish* churlish.

290 *Libany* Libya.

294 *manticors* fabulous ani-
mals supposed to live in India.

296 *Melanchates* the hound
of Actaeon. See Ovid, *Metamorphoses*, i. 163.

Changed to a deer,
The story doth appear,   300
Was changed to an hart :
So thou, foul cat that thou art,
The selfsame hound
Might thee confound,
That his own lorde bote,   305
Might bite asunder thy throat !

    Of Ind the greedy grypes
Might tear out all thy tripes !
Of Arcady the bears
Might pluck away thine ears !   310
The wild wolf Lycaon
Bite asunder thy backbone !
Of Etna the burning hill,
That day and night burneth still,
Set in thy tail a blaze   315
That all the world may gaze
And wonder upon thee,
From Ocean the great sea
Unto the Isles of Orcady,
From Tilbury Ferry   320
To the plain of Salisbury !
So traitorously my bird to kill
That never ought thee evil will !

    Was never bird in cage
More gentle of coráge   325
In doing his homáge
Unto his soveraine.
Alas, I say again,
Death hath departed us twain !
The false cat hath thee slain :   330

---

311 *Lycaon* A king of Ar-
cadia transformed into a wolf
according to the legend recounted
by Ovid in *Metamorphoses*. i.
163 *et seq.*
  319 *Orcady* Orkney.

Farewell, Philip, adew !
Our Lord, thy soul rescue !
Farewell, without restore,
Farewell, for evermore !

And it were a Jew,   335
It would make one rue,
To see my sorrow new.
These villainous false cattès
Were made for mice and rattès,
And not for birdès small.   340
Alas, my face waxeth pale,
Telling this piteous tale,
How my bird so fair,
That was wont to repair,
And go in at my spair,   345
And creep in at my gore
Of my gown before,
Flickering with his wings !
Alas, my heart it stings,
Remembering pretty things !   350
Alas, mine heart it sleth,
My Philip's doleful death !
When I remember it,
How prettily it would sit,
Many times and oft,   355
Upon my finger aloft !
I played with him tittle-tattle,
And fed him with my spittle,
With his bill between my lips,
It was my pretty Phips !   360
Many a pretty kuss
Had I of his sweet muss !

---

345 *spair* opening in a   breast of a gown.
woman's smock or dress.   361 *kuss* kiss.
  346 *gore* opening in the   362 *muss* muzzle, mouth.

And now the cause is thus,
That he is slain me fro,
To my great pain and woe.   365

Of fortune this the chance
Standeth on variance :
Oft time after pleasance
Trouble and grievance.
No man can be sure   370
Always to have pleasure :
As well perceive ye may
How my disport and play
From me was taken away
By Gib, our cat savage,   375
That in a furious rage
Caught Philip by the head
And slew him there stark dead !
    Kyrie, eleison,
    Christe, eleison,   380
    Kyrie, eleison !
For Philip Sparrow's soul,
Set in our bead-roll
Let us now whisper
A Paternoster.   385

    Lauda, anima mea, Dominum !
To weep with me look that ye come
All manner of birdes in your kind ;
See none be left behind.
To mourning looke that ye fall   390
With dolorous songes funerall,
Some to sing, and some to say,
Some to weep, and some to pray.

---

379 *Kyrie, eleison, Christe, eleison* " Lord have mercy, Christ have mercy." Greek prayer used in the Mass and other offices of the Roman Catholic Church.

386 Ps. cxlv in the Vulgate, cxlvi in the A.V.: " Praise ye the Lord, praise the Lord, O my soul.

Every birdè in his lay.
The goldfinch, the wagtail ;   395
The jangling jay to rail,
The fleckèd pie to chatter
Of this dolorous matter ;
And robin red breast,
He shall be the priest   400
The requiem mass to sing,
Softly warbèling,
With the help of the reed sparrow,
And the chatteringe swallow,
This hearse for to hallow ;   405
The lark with his long toe ;
The spink, and the martinet also ;
The shoveller with his broad beak ;
The dotterel, that foolish pek,
And also the mad coot,   410
With a balde face to toot ;
The fieldfare and the snite ;
The crow and the kite ;
The raven, called Rolfè.
His plain-song to sol-fa ;   415
The partridge, the quail ;
The plover with us to wail ;
The woodhack, that singeth ' chur '
Hoarsely, as he had the mur ;
The lusty chanting nightingale ;   420
The popingay to tell her tale,
That toteth oft in a glass,
Shall read the Gospel at mass ;
The mavis with her whistle
Shall read there the pistell.   425

---

407 *spink* chaffinch.
409 *pek* foolish fellow.
411 *toot* pry.
412 *snite* snipe.

418 *woodhack* woodpecker.
419 *mur* cold.
421 *popingay* parrot
424 *mavis* song-thrush
425 *pistell* Epistle.

But with a large and a long
To keepe just plain-song,
Our chanters shall be the cuckowe,
The culver, the stockdowe,
With ' puwit ' the lapwing,   430
The versicles shall sing.

   The bitter with his bumpe,
The crane with his trumpe,
The swan of Menander,
The goose and the gander,   435
The duck and the drake,
Shall watch at this wake ;
The peacock so proud,
Because his voice is loud,
And hath a glorious tail,   440
He shall sing the grail ;
The owl, that is so foul,
Must help us to howl ;
The heron so gaunt,
And the cormorant,   445
With the pheasant,
And the gaggling gant,
And the churlish chough ;
The knot and the ruff ;
The barnacle, the buzzard,   450
With the wild mallard ;
The divendop to sleep ;
The water-hen to weep ;

---

430 *puwit* the cry of the lapwing, mod. " peewit ".

432 *bitter* bittern.

434 *Menander* probably = Mæander, river in Asia Minor famous in classical legend.

441 *grail* graduale, part of the Roman Office for the Dead.

447 *gant* wild goose.

449 old editions read " the rout and the kough ". Mitford first pointed out that this is almost certainly a mistake for " the knout and the rough ", i.e. " the knot and the ruff ".

450 *barnacle* a sort of wild goose.

452 *divendop* dabchick.

The puffin and the teal
Money they shall deal   455
To poore folk at large,
That shall be their charge ;
The seamew and the titmouse ;
The woodcock with the longe nose ;
The throstle with her warbling ;   460
The starling with her brabling ;
The rook, with the osprey
That putteth fishes to a fray ;
And the dainty curlew,
With the turtle most true.   465

   At this *Placebo*
We may not well forgo
The countering of the coe ;
The stork also,
That maketh his nest   470
In chimneys to rest ;
Within those walls
No broken galls
May there abide
Of cuckoldry side,   475
Or else philosophy
Maketh a great lie.
The estridge, that will eat
An horseshoe so great,
In the stead of meat,   480
Such fervent heat
His stomach doth freat ;
He cannot well fly,
Nor sing tunably,
Yet at a brayd   485
He hath well assayed

468 *countering* answering ; *coe* jackdaw.
469 The stork was a bird of good omen and was supposed to forsake a house if adultery was committed in it.

478 *estridge* ostrich.

To sol-fa above E-la.
Fa, lorell, fa, fa !
Ne quando
Male cantando,   490
The best that we can,
To make him our bell-man,
And let him ring the bells,
He can do nothing else.

          Chaunticlere, our cock,   495
Must tell what is of the clock
By the astrology
That he hath naturally
Conceived and caught,
And was never taught   500
By Albumazer
The astronomer,
Nor by Ptolomy
Prince of astronomy,
Nor yet by Haly ;   505
And yet he croweth daily
And nightly the tides
That no man abides,
With Partlot his hen,
Whom now and then   510
He plucketh by the head
When he doth her tread.

     The bird of Araby,
     That potentially

489, 490 *Ne quando*, etc. lest
sometimes by singing ill.
501 *Albumazer* Arabian
astronomer of the ninth century
A.D.

503 *Ptolomy : Claudius Pto-
lemaeus* Egyptian astronomer of
the second century A.D.
505 *Haly* Arabian astronomer, flourished *c.* A.D. 1199.

May never die,   515
And yet there is none
But one alone ;
A phoenix it is
This hearse that must bless
With aromatic gummès.   520
That cost great summès,
The way of thurification
To make a fumigation,
Sweet of reflare,
And redolent of aire,   525
This corse for to cense
With greate reverence,
As patriarch or pope
In a blackè cope.
While he censeth the hearse,   530
He shall sing the verse,
Libera me,
In *de la*, *sol*, *re*,
Softly B molle
For my sparrow's soulè.   535
Pliny sheweth all
In his story natural
What he doth find
Of the phoenix kind ;
Of whose incineration   540
There riseth a new creation
Of the same fashion
Without alteration,
Saving that olde age
Is turned into corage   545

---

522 *thurification* burning of incense.

524 *reflare* scent.

529 *blackè cope* black cope worn by the priest at the Absolution over the tomb.

532 *Libera me* antiphon from the Roman Office for the Dead : " Deliver me, O Lord ".

536 *Pliny* Pliny describes the Phoenix in his *Historia Naturalis*, Bk. X.

Of fresh youth again ;
This matter true and plain,
Plain matter indeed,
Who so list to read.

But for the eagle doth fly   550
Highest in the sky,
He shall be the sedean,
The choir to demean,
As provost principal,
To teach them their ordinal ;   555
Also the noble falcon,
With the gerfawcon,
The tarsel gentil,
They shall mourn soft and still
In their amice of gray ;   560
The sacre with them shall say
Dirige for Philip's soul ;
The goshawk shall have a roll
The choristers to control ;
The lanners and the merlions   565
Shall stand in their mourning-gowns ;
The hobby and the musket
The censers and the cross shall fet ;
The kestrel in all this wark
Shall be holy water clerk.   570

---

552 *sedean* sub-dean or sub-deacon.

557 *gerfawcon* a kind of large falcon.

558 *tarsel gentil* tercel-gentle, the male of the falcon.

560 *amice* " an article of costume of the religious orders lined with grey fur " (*N.E.D.*).

561 *sacre* a kind of large falcon. The modern form is " saker ".

565 *lanners* " a species of falcon found in countries bordering on the Mediterranean " (*N.E.D.*) ; *merlions* merlins, " a European species of falcon " (*N.E.D.*).

567 *hobby* " a small species of falcon " (*N.E.D.*) ; *musket* " a small kind of sparrow hawk " (*N.E.D.*).

568 *fet* fetched.

569 *wark* work.

And now the dark cloudy night
Chaseth away Phoebus bright,
Taking his course toward the west,
God send my sparrow's soul good rest !
Requiem aeternam dona eis, Domine !   575
Fa, fa, fa, mi, re, re.
A por ta in fe ri,
Fa, fa, fa, mi, mi.

   Credo videre bona Domini,
I pray God, Philip to heaven may fly !   580
Domine, exaudi orationem meam !
To heaven he shall, from heaven he came !
   Do mi nus vo bis cum !
Of all good prayers God send him some !
   Oremus,   585
Deus, cui proprium est misereri et parcere,
On Philip's soul have pity !
For he was a pretty cock,
And came of a gentle stock,
And wrapt in a maiden's smock,   590
And cherished full daintily,
Till cruel fate made him to die :
Alas, for doleful destiny !
But whereto should I
Longer mourn or cry ?   595
To Jupiter I call,
Of heaven imperiall,

---

575 *Requiem aeternam*, etc. "Give them eternal rest, O Lord". Verse sung at the end of each psalm in the Office for the Dead.

579 *Credo videre bona Domini* "I believe that I see the blessings of the Lord". Antiphon from the form of the Office for the Dead found in the Sarum Breviary.

585–6 *Oremus*, etc. "Let us pray", the command at the end of the Office for the Dead followed by the *Oratio*: *Deus, cui proprium*, etc. "God, whose nature it is to pity and to spare". The lines that follow in the text are a somewhat irreverent parody of this prayer.

That Philip may fly
Above the starry sky,
To tread the pretty wren,   600
That is our Lady's hen.
Amen, amen, amen !

    Yet one thing is behind,
That now cometh to mind ;
An epitaph I would have   605
For Philippès grave ;
But for I am a maid,
Timorous, half afraid,
That never yet assayed
Of Heliconès well,   610
Where the Muses dwell ;
Though I can read and spell,
Recount, report, and tell
Of the Tales of Canterbury,
Some sad stories, some merry ;   615
As Palamon and Arcet,
Duke Theseus, and Partelet ;
And of the Wife of Bath,
That worketh much scath
When her tale is told   620
Among the housewives bold,
How she controlled
Her husbands as she wold,
And them to despise
In the homeliest wise,   625
Bring other wives in thought
Their husbands to set at nought.
And though that read have I
Of Gawain and Sir Guy,
And tell can a great piece   630
Of the Golden Fleece,
How Jason it wan,
Like a valiant man ;

Of Arthur's Round Table,
With his knights commendáble,   635
And Dame Gaynour, his queen,
Was somewhat wanton, I ween ;
How Sir Lancelot de Lake
Many a spear brake
For his lady's sake ;   640
Of Tristram, and King Mark,
And all the whole wark
Of Belle Isold his wife,
For whom was much strife ;
Some say she was light,   645
And made her husband knight
Of the common hall,
That cuckolds men call ;
And of Sir Lybius,
Named Dysconius ;   650
Of *Quater Fylz Amund,*
And how they were summoned
To Rome, to Charlemagne,
Upon a great pain,
And how they rode each one   655
On Bayard Mountalbon ;
Men see him now and then
In the forest of Ardén.
What though I can frame
The stories by name   660
Of Judas Maccabeus,
And of Caesar Julius ;
And of the love between
Paris and Vienne ;

---

636 *Gaynour* Guenevere.
649, 650 *Sir Lybius Dys-*
conius famous medieval romance, see below p. 81 n.
651 *Quater Fylz Amund*
"The Four Sons of Aymon", a

famous medieval romance of the
Charlemagne cycle translated by
Caxton.
664 *Paris and Vienne* another medieval romance also
translated by Caxton.

And of the duke Hannibal,   665
That made the Romans all
Fordread and to quake ;
How Scipion did wake
The city of Cartháge,
Which by his unmerciful rage   670
He beat down to the ground
And though I can expound
Of Hector of Troy,
That was all their joy,
Whom Achilles slew,   675
Wherefore all Troy did rue ;
And of the love so hot
That made Troilus to dote
Upon fair Cresseid ;
And what they wrote and said,   680
And of their wanton willés
Pander bare the billés
From one to the other ;
His master's love to further,
Sometime a precious thing,   685
An ouche or else a ring ;
From her to him again
Sometime a pretty chain,
Or a bracelet of her hair,
Prayed Troilus for to wear   690
That token for her sake ;
How heartily he did it take,
And much thereof did make ;
And all that was in vain,
For she did but feign ;   695
The story telleth plain,
He could not obtain,

---

678 *Troilus*   see   Chaucer's   686 *ouche* jewel.
Troilus and Criseyde.

Though his father were a king,
Yet there was a thing
That made the male to wring ;   700
She made him to sing
The song of lover's lay ;
Musing night and day,
Mourning all alone,
Comfort had he none,   705
For she was quite gone,
Thus in conclusion,
She brought him in abusion ;
In earnest and in game
She was much to blame ;   710
Disparaged is her fame,
And blemished is her name,
In manner half with shame ;
Troilus also hath lost
On her much love and cost,   715
And now must kiss the post ;
Pandarus, that went between,
Hath won nothing, I ween,
But light for summer green ;
Yet for a special laud   720
He is named Troilus' bawd ;
Of that name he is sure
Whilès the world shall dure.

      Though I remember the fable
Of Penelope most stable,   725
To her husband most true,
Yet long-time she ne knew
Whether he were live or dead ;
Her wit stood her in stead,

---

700 *male to wring* the meaning is obscure. male=wallet.

That she was true and just   730
For any bodily lust
To Ulysses her make,
And never would him forsake.

Of Marcus Marcellus
A process I could tell us ;   735
And of Antiochus,
And of Josephus
De Antiquitatibus ;
And of Mardocheus,
And of great Ahasuerus,   740
And of Vesca his queen,
Whom he forsook with teen,
And of Esther his other wife,
With whom he led a pleasant life ;
Of King Alexander ;   745
And of King Evander ;
And of Porsena the great,
That made the Romans to sweat.

Though I have enrolled
A thousand new and old   750
Of these historious tales,
To fill budgets and males

---

734 *Marcus Marcellus* Roman general killed by Hannibal in the Second Punic War.

736 *Antiochus* the wicked king of Antioch in the medieval romance of Apollonius of Tyre. The story is used by Gower in his *Confessio Amantis* and by Shakespeare in *Pericles*.

737, 738 *Josephus De Antiquitatibus* the reference is to Flavius Josephus, the Jewish historian of the first century A.D., one of whose works is entitled *De Antiquitatibus Judaeorum*.

739 *Mardocheus* Mordecai, see the *Book of Esther*.

741 *Vesca* Vashti.

746 *Evander* see Virgil, *Aeneid*, VIII.

747 *Porsena* Etruscan king described by Livy. See Macaulay's *Lays of Ancient Rome*.

With books that I have read,
Yet I am nothing sped,
And can but little skill   755
Of Ovid or Virgil,
Or of Plutarch,
Or Francis Petrarch,
Alcaeus or Sappho,
Or such other poets mo,   760
As Linus and Homerus,
Euphorion and Theocritus,
Anacreon and Arion,
Sophocles and Philemon,
Pindarus and Simonides,   765
Philistion and Pherecydes ;
These poets of ancienté,
They are too diffuse for me :

    For, as I tofore have said,
I am but a young maid,   770
And cannot in effect
My style as yet direct
With English words elect.
Our natural tongue is rude,
And hard to be ennewed   775
With polished termés lusty ;
Our language is so rusty,
So cankered, and so full
Of frowardés, and so dull,
That if I would apply   780
To write ornatelý,
I wot not where to find
Termés to serve my mind.

759–66 *Alcaeus . . . Phere-cydes*. These writers could only have been known by name to Skelton. Linus is a mythical figure and Pherecydes of Syros was not a poet but an early Greek philosopher.

Gower's English is old,
And of no value told ;   785
His matter is worth gold,
And worthy to be enrolled.

In Chaucer I am sped,
His tales I have read ;
His matter is delectable,   790
Solacious, and commendable ;
His English well allowed,
So as it is enprowed,
For as it is employed
There is no English void,   795
At those days much commended :
And now men would have amended
His English, whereat they bark,
And mar all they wark.
Chaucer, that famous clerk,   800
His termés were not dark,
But pleasant, easy, and plain ;
No word he wrote in vain.

Also John Lydgáte
Writeth after an higher rate ;   805
It is diffuse to find
The sentence of his mind,
Yet writeth he in his kind,
No man that can amend
Those matters that he hath penned ;   810
Yet some men find a faute,
And say he writeth too haute.
Wherefore hold me excused
If I have not well perused
Mine English half abused ;   815
Though it be refused,
In worth I shall it take,
And fewer wordes make.

But, for my sparrow's sake,
Yet as a woman may,   820
My wit I shall assay
An epitaph to write
In Latin plain and light,
Whereof the elegy
Followeth by and by :   825

Flos volucrum formose, vale !   Philippe, sub isto
 Marmore jam recubas, qui mihi carus eras.
Semper erunt nitido radiantia sidera cœlo ;
 Impressusque meo pectore semper eris.

*   *

826–9 This Latin epitaph in elegiac verse can be translated
as follows :

Beautiful flower of birds, farewell, O sparrow now lying
 Under a marble stone, dear to me, Philip, alone.
Always the radiant stars will shine in the glorious heavens,
 Always thy image will rest, Philip, engraved on my breast.

VII

THE TUNNING OF
ELINOUR RUMMING

(Extracts)

I

Tell you I chill,   1
If that ye will
A while be still
Of a comely gill
That dwelt on a hill :   5
But she is not gryll,
For she is somewhat sage
And well worn in age.
For her visage
It would asswage   10
A mannés courage,
    Her loathly leare
Is nothing clear,
But ugly of cheer,
Droop and drowsy,   15
Scurvy and lowsy,
Her face all bowsy,
Comely crinkled,
Woundrously wrinkled,
Like a roast piggès ear,   20
Bristled with hair.

    Her lewd lippes twain,
They slaver, men sain,
Like a ropy rain,

1	*I chill* Ich will, i.e. I will.	12	*leare* complexion.
4	*gill* Jill, i.e. woman.	23	*sain* say.
6	*gryll* fierce.	24	*ropy* sticky, stringy.

72

A gummy glair.   25
She is ugly fair.
Her nose somedele hookèd,
And camously crooked,
Never stopping,
But ever dropping ;   30
Her skin, loose and slack,
Grainèd like a sack ;
With a crooked back.
   Her eyen gowndy
Are full unsowndy,   35
For they are bleared ;
And she gray-haired,
Jawed like a jetty ;
A man would have pity
To see how she is gummèd,   40
Fingered and thumbèd,
Gently jointed,
Greased and anointed
Up to the knuckles ;
The bones of her huckles   45
Like as they were with buckles
Together made fast.
Her youth is far past.
Footed like a plane,
Legged like a crane,   50
And yet she will jet
Like a jolly fet,
In her furred flocket,
And gray russet rocket,

---

25 *glair* viscous matter.
27 *somedele* somewhat.
28 *camously* from camois =
having a pug-nose.
34 *gowndy* bleared.
38 *jetty* projecting part of a
building.

45 *huckles* hips. M. reads
" legges ".
51 *jet* swagger.
52 *jolly fet* handsome
woman.
53, 54 *flocket . . . rocket*
women's garments.

With simper the cocket.   55
Her hood of Lincoln green
It had been hers, I ween,
More than forty year ;
And so doth it appear,
For the green bare threads   60
Look like sere weeds,
Withered like hay,
The wool worn away.
And yet, I dare say,
She thinketh herself gay   65
Upon the holy day
When she doth her array
And girdeth in her getes.
Stitched and pranked with pleats ;
Her kirtle Bristow-red.   70
With clothes upon her head
That weigh a sow of lead
Writeth in wonder wise
After the Saracen's guise,
With a whim-wham   75
Knit with a trim-tram
Upon her brain-pan ;
Like an Egyptian
Capped about.
When she goeth out   80
Herself for to shew,
She driveth down the dew.
With a pair of heeles
As broad as two wheeles ;
She hobbles as a goose   85
With her blanket hose

---

55 *simper the cocket* a term still used in Elizabethan times for a simpering coquette.

68 *getes* clothes.

70 *Bristow* Bristol.

72 *sow* " a large oblong mass of solidified metal " (*N.E.D.*).

76 *trim-tram* ornament.

78 *Egyptian* gipsy.

Over the fallow ;
Her shoon smeared with tallow,
Greased upon dirt
That baudeth her skirt.   90

II

Instead of coin and money   1
Some bringe her a coney,
And some a pot with honey,
Some a salt, and some a spoon,
Some their hose, some their shoon ;   5
Some run a good trot
With a skillet or a pot ;
Some fill their pot full
Of good Lemster wool :
An housewife of trust,   10
When she is athirst,
Such a web can spin,
Her thrift is full thin.

Some go straight thither,
Be it slaty or slider :   15
They hold the high way
They care not what men say,
Be that as be may.
Some, loth to be espied,
Start in at the backe side   20
Over the hedge and pale,
And all for the good ale.
Some run till they sweat,
Bring with them malt or wheat,

---

90 *baudeth* fouls.
2   *coney* rabbit.
4   *salt* salt-cellar.
7   *skillet* small kettle.

9 *Lemster* Leominster in
Herefordshire, famous for its
wool.
15 *slaty* muddy ; *slider*
slippery.

And dame Elinour entreat   25
To birle them of the best.

　　Then cometh an other guest :
She sweareth by the rood of rest
Her lippes are so dry
Without drink she must die,   30
Therefore fill it by and by,
And have here a peck of rye.

　　Anon cometh another,
As dry as the other,
And with her doth bring   35
Meal, salt, or other thing,
Her harvest girdle, her wedding-ring,
To pay for her scot
As cometh to her lot.
One bringeth her husband's hood   40
Because the ale is good ;
Another brought her his cap
To offer to the ale-tap,
With flax and with tow ;
And some brought sour dough   45
With ' Hey ' and with ' ho ! '
Sit we down a row,
And drink till we blow,
And pipe tirly tyrlow !

　　Some laid to pledge   50
Their hatchet and their wedge,
Their heckle and their reel,
Their rock, their spinning-wheel ;

26　*birle*　pour out.
28　*rood*　cross.
37　*harvest girdle*　" perhaps a girdle worn at the feast after the gathering in of the corn".—D.

38　*scot*　reckoning.
52　*heckle*　comb for dressing flax.
53　*rock*　spindle

And some went so narrow
They laid to pledge their wharrow,   55
Their ribskin and their spindle,
Their needle and their thimble.
Here was scant thrift
When they made such shift.
   Their thirst was so great   60
They asked never for meat,
But ' Drink, still drink,
And let the cat wink !
Let us wash our gums
From the dry crumbs ! '   65

---

55 *wharrow* a grooved pul-
ley in a spinning wheel.

56 *ribskin* probably a leather
apron.

VIII

AGAINST THE SCOTS

(Extract)

Against the proud Scots clattering,   1
That never will leave their tratling :
Won they the field, and lost their king ?
They may well say, fie on that winning !

    Lo, these fond sots   5
    And tratling Scots,
    How they are blind
    In their own mind,
    And will not know
    Their overthrow   10
    At Branxton Moor !
    They are so stour,
    So frantic mad,
    They say they had
    And won the field   15
    With spear and shield.
    That is as true
    As black is blue
    And green is grey !
    Whatever they say,   20
    Jemmy is dead
    And closed in lead,
    That was their own king :
    Fie on that winning !

---

2 *tratling* prattling.

11 *Branxton* village in Northumberland near which the
battle of Flodden was fought.

12 *stour* obstinate.

21 *Jemmy* James IV of
Scotland, killed at the battle of
Flodden, 9 Sept. 1513.

At Flodden hills   25
Our bows, our bills,
Slew all the floure
Of their honour.
Are not these Scots
Fools and sots,   30
Such boast to make,
To prate and crake,
To face, to brace,
All void of grace,
So proud of heart,   35
So overthwart,
So out of frame,
So void of shame,
As it is enrolled,
Written and told   40
Within this quaire ?
Who list to repair,
And therein read,
Shall find indeed
A mad reckoning,   45
Considering all thing,
That the Scots may sing
Fie on the winning !

---

32 *crake* vaunt.   36 *overthwart* perverse.
33 *brace* brag.   41 *quaire* book.

IX

AGAINST GARNESCHE

SKELTON LAUREATE, DEFENDER, AGAINST MASTER GARNESCHE, CHALLENGER

Sith ye have me challenged, Master Garnesche,　　　　1
　　Rudely reviling me in the king's noble hall,
Such another challenger could no man wish,
　　But if it were Sir Termagant that tourneyed without
　　　　nall ;
　　For Sir Frollo de Franko was never half so tall.　　5
But say me now, Sir Satrapas, what authority ye have
In your challenge, Sir Chesten, to call me a knave ?

What, have ye kithed you a knight, Sir Douglas the
　　　　Doughty,
　　So currishly to beknave me in the king's palace ?
Ye strong sturdy stallion, so stern and stouty,　　　10
　　Ye bear ye bold as Barabas, or Sir Terry of Thrace ;
　　Ye girn grimly with your gummès and with your grisly
　　　　face !
But say me yet, Sir Satrapas, what authority ye have
In your challenge, Sir Chesten, to call me a knave ?

---

4 *Termagant* an imaginary furious deity whom the Saracens were (falsely) supposed to worship ; *nall* Middle English for "awl". The meaning perhaps is that he had no point to his weapon.

5 *Frollo de Franko* a Roman knight, governor of Gaul, slain by King Arthur, according to Geoffrey of Monmouth.

6, 7, 11, 16 *Sir Satrapas, Sir Chesten, Sir Terry, Sir captain of Catywade.* Invented names.

8 *kithed you* made yourself known ; *Sir Douglas* see Shakespeare, *Henry IV*, pt. I.

12 *girn* grin.

Ye foul, fierce and fell, as Sir Ferumbras the freke,   15
   Sir captain of Catywade, catacumbas of Cayre,
Though ye be lusty as Sir Libius lances to break,
   Yet your countenance uncomely, your face is not fair ;
   For all your proud pranking, your pride may apayr,
But say me yet, Sir Satrapas, what authority ye have   20
In your challenge, Sir Chesten, to call me a knave ?

Of Mantrible the Bridge, Malchus the Murrion,
   Nor black Balthasar with his basnet rough as a bear,
Nor Lycaon, that loathly lusk, in mine opinion,
   Nor no boar so brimly bristled is with hair,   25
   As ye are bristled on the back for all your gay gear.
But say me yet, Sir Satrapas, what authority ye have
In your challenge, Sir Chesten, to call me a knave ?

Your wind-shaken shanks, your long loathly legs,
   Crooked as a camock, and as a cow calfless,   30
Brings you out of favour with all female tegs ;
   That Mistress Punt put you off, it was not all causeless;
   At Orwell her haven your anger was lawless.
But say me yet, Sir Satrapas, what authority ye have
In your challenge, Sir Chesten, to call me a knave ?   35

I say, ye solemn Saracen, all black is your ble ;
   As a glede glowing, your eyen glister as glass,

---

15 *Sir Ferumbras the freke* Ferumbras was a famous giant in the Charlemagne romances who is vanquished by Oliver. "freke" is a man or warrior.

16 *catacumbas of Cayre* Catacombs of Cairo.

17 *Sir Libius* the hero of the romance *Lybeaus Disconus* (le beau desconnu).

22 *Mantrible : Malchus* the reference is to the bridge Man-

trible in Caxton's *Charles the Great* (translation of romance of Charlemagne) which was guarded by a giant ; *Murrion* Moor.

24 *lusk* a vile person, knave.

25 *brimly* fiercely.

30 *camock* a crooked stick.

31 *tegs* midland word for a sheep, perhaps used here facetiously for women.

33 *Orwell* in Suffolk.

36 *ble* colour, complexion.

J.S.—6

Rolling in your hollow head, ugly to see ;
   Your teeth tainted with tawny ; your snivelly snout
      doth pass,
   Hooked as an hawkès beak, like Sir Topas.   40
Boldly bend you to battle, and busk yourself to save :
Challenge yourself for a fool, call me no more knave !

     By the King's most noble commandment.

            *   *

X

From MAGNIFICENCE

(Extracts)

1. FANCY'S HAWK

Lo this is   1
My fancy, I wis.
Now Christ it, blessé
It is by Jessé

A bird full sweet,   5
For me full meet :
She is furred for the heat
All to the feet ;

Her browés bent,
Her eyen glent :   10
From Tyne to Trent,
From Stroud to Kent.

A man shall find
Many of her kind.
How stand the wind   15
Before or behind ?

Barbéd like a nun,
For burning of the sun ;
Her feathers dun ;
Well favoured bonne.   20

---

10 *glent* glowing, lustrous.   of a nun.
17 *barbéd* wearing a " barb "   20 *bonne* good girl.
or white linen headdress like that

83

Now let me see about
In all this rout
If I can find out
So seemly a snout.

Among this press :   25
Even a whole mess—
Peace, man, peace !
I rede, we cease.

So farly fair as it lookès,
And her beak so comely crookès   30
Her nailes sharp as tenter hookès !
I have not kept her yet three wookès.

And how still she does sit !
Te whit, te whit, where is my wit ?

2. ADVERSITY SPEAKS

I am Adversity, that for thy misdeed   1
From God am sent to quit thee thy meed.
Vile vilyard, thou must not now my dint withstand,
Thou must abide the dint of my hand :
Ly there, losel, for all thy pomp and pride ;   5
Thy pleasure now with pain and trouble shall be tried.
The stroke of God, Adversity I hight ;
I pluck doun king, prince, lord and knight,
I rush at them roughly and make them lie full low,
And in their most trust I make them overthrow   10

---

28 *rede* advise.
29 *farly* wondrous.
32 *wookès* weeks.
Adversity Speaks. The stage
direction is " here Magnificence
is beaten down, and spoiled from

all his goods and raiment ".
  2 *meed* desert.
  3 *vilyard* vile fellow ; *dint*
stroke.
  5 *losel* profligate.
  7 *hight* am called.

This losel was a lord, and lived at his lust,
And now like a lurden, he lieth in the dust.
He knew not himself, his heart was so high ;
Now there is no man that will set by him a fly :
He was wont to boast, brag, and to brace,   15
Now dare he not for shame look one in the face.
All worldly wealth for him too little was ;
Now hath he right nought, naked as an ass :
Sometime without measure he trusted in gold,
And now without measure he shall have hunger and
    cold.   20
Lo, sirs, thus I handle them all
That follow their fancies in folly to fall :
Man or woman, of what estate they be,
I counsel them beware of Adversity.

3. LIBERTY'S SONG

With, yea marry, sirs, thus should it be.   1
I kist her sweet, and she kissed me ;
I dancèd the darling on my knee ;
I garred her gasp, I garred her glee,
With dance on the lea, the lea !   5
I bussèd that baby with heart so free ;
She is the boot of all my bale ;
A, so, that sigh was far fet !
To love that lovesome I will not let ;
My heart is wholly on her set :   10
I plucked her by the patlet ;
At my device I with her met ;
My fancy fairly on her I set ;
So merely singeth the nightingale !
In lust and liking my name is Liberty.   15

---

12 *lurden* vagabond.   7 *boot* cure ; *bale* misfortune
4 *garred* made, caused ; *glee*   9 *let* cease.
rejoice.
6 *bussèd* kissed.   11 *patlet* dress.

I am desired with highest and lowest degree ;
I lived as me list, I leap out at large ;
Of earthly thing I have no care nor charge ;
I am president of princes, I prick them with pride :
What is he living that liberty would lack ?   20
A thousand pound with liberty may hold no tack ;
At liberty a man may be bold for to break ;
Wealth without liberty, goeth all to wrack,
But yet, sirs, hardily one thing learn of me :
I warn you beware of too much liberty,   25
For *totum in toto* is not worth an haw ;
Too hardy, or too much, too free of the daw ;
Too sober, too sad, too subtle, too wise ;
Too merry, too mad, too giggling, too nice ;
Too full of fancies, too lordly, too proud ;   30
Too homely, too holy, too lewd, and too loud,
Too flattering, too smattering, too, too out of harre,
Too clattering, too chattering, too short, and too far,
Too jetting, too jagging, and too full of japes
Too mocking, too mowing, too like a jackanapes   35
Thus *totum in toto* groweth up, as ye may see,
By means of madness, and too much liberty
For I am a virtue, if I be well used,
And I am a vice where I am abused.

4. GOODHOPE AND MAGNIFICENCE

(*Magnificence is about to kill himself when Goodhope
appears and snatches away his sword*)

Good :   Alas, dear son, sore cumbered is thy mind,   1
          Thyself that thou would slo against nature and
          kind !

---

26 *totum in toto* all in all ;
haw   hawthorn-berry, hence
something of no value.
27 *daw* playing the fool.

32 *out of harre* out of joint.
34 *jagging* thrusting, slash-
ing.
2 *slo* slay.

Magn : Ah, blessèd may ye be, sir ! What shall I you
       call ?
Good : Goodhope, sir, my name is ; remedy principall
       Against all sautès of your gostly foe :   5
       Who knoweth me, himself may never slo.
Magn : Alas, sir, I am lappèd in adversity,
       That despair well nigh hath mischievèd me
       For, had ye not the sooner been my refuge,
       Of damnation I had been drawn in the luge.   10
Good : Undoubted ye had not lost yourself eternally :
       There is no man may sin more mortally
       Than of wanhope through the unhappy ways,
       By mischief to breviate and shorten his days :
       But my good son, learn from despair to flee,   15
       Wind you from wanhope, and acquaint you with
          me
       A great misadventure, thy Maker to displease
       Thyself mischieving to thine endless disease !
       There was never so hard a storm of misery,
       But through goodhope there may come remedy.
Magn : Your words be more sweeter than any precious
          nard,   21
       They mollify so easily my heart that was so hard;
       There is no balm, ne gum of Araby
       More delectable than your language to me.
Good : Sir, your physician is the grace of God.   25

---

5 *sautès* assaults.

10 *luge* lodge.

14 *breviate* abbreviate.

16 *wanhope* despair.

21 *more sweeter* double comparative, common in Tudor English.

XI

COLIN CLOUT

(Extracts)

Quis consurget mecum adversus malignantes? Aut quis stabit mecum adversus operantes iniquitatem? Nemo, Domine!

I

What can it avail   1
To drive forth a snail,
Or to make a sail
Of an herring's tail?
To rhyme or to rail,   5
To write or to indite,
Either for delite
Or else for despite?
Or bookès to compile
Of divers manner style,   10
Vice to revile
And sin to exile?
To teach or to preach,
As reason will reach?
Say this, and say that,   15
His head is so fat,
He wotteth never what
Nor whereof he speaketh;
He crieth and he creaketh,
He prieth and he peketh,   20

88

He chides and he chatters,
He prates and he patters,
He clitters and he clatters,
He meddles and he smatters,
He gloses and he flatters ;   25
Or if he speak plain,
Then he lacketh brain,
He is but a fool ;
Let him go to school,
On three-footed stool   30
That he may down sit,
For he lacketh wit !
And if that he hit
The nail on the head,
It standeth in no stead.   35
The devil, they say, is dead
The devil is dead !

It may well so be,
Or else they would see
Otherwise, and flee   40
From worldly vanity,
And foul covetousness,
And other wretchedness,
Fickle falseness,
Variableness,   45
With unstableness.

And if ye stand in doubt
Who brought this ryme about,
My name is Colin Clout.
I purpose to shake out   50
All my conning bag.
Like a clerkly hag,

---

51   *conning bag*   store of learning.

For though my rhyme be ragged,
Tatteréd and jaggéd,
Rudely rain-beaten,   55
Rusty and moth-eaten,
If ye take well therewith,
It hath in it some pith.
For, as far as I can see,
It is wrong with each degree :   60
For the temporality
Accuseth the spirituality ;
The spiritual again
Doth grudge and complain
Upon the temporal men :   65
Thus, each of other bloder
The t'one against t'oder
Alas, they make me shoder !
For in hoder moder
The church is put in fault ;   70
The prelates ben so haut,
They say, and look so high,
As though they wouldé fly
Above the starry sky.

II

Thus I, Colin Clout,   1
As I go about,
And wandering as I walk
I hear the people talk.
Men say, for silver and gold   5
Mitres are bought and sold ;
There shall no clergy appose

---

66 *bloder* blether.
67 *t'oder* the other.
68 *shoder* shudder.
69 *hoder moder* hugger mugger.

71 *haut* haughty.
7 *clergy* learning ; *appose* lit. confront or examine, here apparently = obtain.

A mitre nor a crose,
But a full purse :
A straw for Goddės curse !   10
What are they the worse ?
For a simoniac
Is but a hermoniac ;
And no more ye make
Of simony, men say,   15
But a childės play.

   Over this, the foresaid lay,
Reporte how the Pope may
An holy anchor call
Out of the stonė wall,   20
And him a bishop make,
If he on him can take
To keep so hard a rule
To ride upon a mule
With golde all betrappéd,   25
In purple and pall belapped ;
Some hatted and some capped,
Richly and warm bewrapped,
God wot to their great pains !
In rochets of fine Rennes,   30
White as morrowe's milk ;
Their tabards of fine silk,
Their stirrups of mixt gold begared :
There may no cost be spared,

8 *mitre . . . crose* a bishopric
or an abbey.

12 *simoniac* one who ob-
tains ecclesiastical preferment by
corrupt means. See Acts viii.
18, 19.

13 *hermoniac* possibly from
Hermes, who was god of thieves,
or from Hermes Trismegistus,
reputed to be a magician and
hence a charlatan. A third possi-
bility is that it is a form of
" armoniac " or " ammoniac ",
a purgative medicine.

19 *anchor* anchorite.

28 D's reading from MS. K.
has " Richely bewrapped ".

30 *rochets* vestments.

32 *tabards* loose garments.

33 *begared* adorned.

Their mulês gold doth eat,   35
Their neighbours die for meat.
    What care they though Gil sweat,
Or Jack of the Noke ?
The poore people they yoke
With summons and citations   40
And excommunications,
About churches and markét,
The bishop on his carpét
At home full soft doth sit,
This is a farly fit,   45
To hear the people jangle,
How warlike they wrangle.
Alas, why do ye not handle
And them all to-mangle ?
Full falsely on you they lie,   50
And shamefully you ascry,
And say as untruely
As the butterfly,
A man might say in mock,
Ware the weathercock   55
Of the steeple of Poulês.
And thus they hurt their soulês
In slandering you for truth.
Alas, it is great ruth !
Some say yet sit in thronês,   60
Like princes *aquilonis*,
And shrine your rotten bonês
With pearls and precious stonês ;
But how the commons groans,
And the people moans   65

---

37 *Gil* and 38 *Jack of the*
Noke names for common people.
Jack of the Noke is probably
" Jack of the Oak ".
  45 *farly* K. reads " fearful ".

51 *ascry* cry out against,
attack.
56 *Poulês* St. Paul's.
61 *princes aquilonis* princes
of the North, i.e. Lucifers.

For prestès and for loans
Lent and never paid,
But from day to day delayed,
The commonwealth decayed,
Men say ye are tongue-tied,   70
And thereof speak nothing
But dissimuling and glosing.

III

And all the fault they lay   1
On you, prelates, and say
Ye do them wrong and no right
To put them thus to flight ;
No matins at midnight,   5
Book and chalice gone quite ;
And pluck away the leads
Even over their heads,
And sell away their bells,
And all that they have else !   10
Thus the people tells,
Railès like rebéls,
Redes shrewdly and spells,
And with foundations mells,
And talks like titivels,   15
How ye brake the deadès wills,
Turn monasteries into water-mills ;
Of an abbey ye make a grange ;
Your works, they say, are strange ;
So that their founders' souls   20
Have lost their beadèrolls,
The money for their masses
Spent among wanton lasses ;

---

66 *prestès* advances of money.   15 *titivels* frantic fools. Titi-
67 *paid* repaid.   vellius is the name of a devil in
1 *the fault* K. omits.   the Miracle and Morality plays.
13 *redes* takes counsel.   18 *ye* so M.   K. reads
                                      " they ".

The *diriges* are forgotten ;
Their founders lie there rotten,   25
But where their soulès dwell,
Therewith I will not mell.
What could the Turk do more
With all his false lore,
Turk, Saracen, or Jew !   30
I report me to you,
O merciful Jesu,
You support and rescue,
My style for to direct,
It may take some effect !   35
For I abhor to write
How the laity despite
You prelates, that of right
Should be lanterns of light.

IV

But now my mind ye understand,   1
For they must take in hand
To preach, and to withstand
All manner of objections ;
For bishops have protections,   5
They say, to do corrections,
But they have no affections
To take the said directions.
In such manner of cases,
Men say, they bear no faces   10
To occupy such places,
To sow the seed of graces :
Their heartès are so fainted,
And they be so attainted

---

24 *diriges*: *Dirige* (*me do-mine*), "Lead me O Lord", Ps. v. 8, used as an antiphon in the Roman Office for the Dead.
7 *affections* K. " afflec-tions ".

With covetise and ambition,   15
And other superstition,
That they be deaf and dumb,
And play silence and glum,
Can say nothing but " mum."

They occupy them so   20
With singing *placebo*,
They will no farther go :
They had liefer to please,
And take their worldly ease,
Than to take on hand   25
Worshipfully to withstand
Such temporal war and hate
As now is made of late
Against Holy Church estate,
Or to maintain good quarréls.   30
The lay men call them barréls,
Full of gluttony
And of hypocrisy,
That counterfeits and paints,
As they were very saints.   35
In matters that them like
They shew them politic.
Pretending gravity
And signiority,
With all solemnity,   40
For their indemnity !
For they will have no loss
Of a penny nor of a cross
Of their predial lands,
That cometh to their hands,   45
And as far as they dare set,
All is fish that cometh to net.

---

18 *glum* a sullen look.   43 *cross* coin marked with
                                     a cross.
21 *placebo* see p. 44 n.   44 *predial lands* farm lands.

Building royally
Their mansions curiously,
With turrets and with towers,   50
With hallès and with bowers,
Stretching to the stars,
With glass windows and bars ;
Hanging about the walles
Cloths of gold and palles,   55
Arras of rich array,
Fresh as flowers in May ;
With dame Diana naked ;
How lusty Venus quaked,
And how Cupid shaked   60
His dart, and bent his bow
For to shoot a crow
At her tirly tirlow ;
And how Paris of Troy
Danced a *lege de moy*,   65
Made lusty sport and joy
With dame Helen the queen ;
With such stories bydene
Their chambers well be seen,
With triumphs of Caesar,   70
And of Pompeius' war,
Of renown and of fame,
By them to get a name.
Now all the worlde stares,
How they ride in goodly chairs,   75
Conveyed by elephants,
With laureate garlants,
And by unicornès
With their seemly hornès ;
Upon these beastes riding.   80
Naked boyes striding,

---

65 *lege de moy* a dance.   70 *triumphs*, etc. actual
                                     sets of tapestries at Hampton
68 *bydene* by the dozen.   Court Palace.

With wanton wenches winking,
Now truly, to my thinking,
That is a speculation
And a meet meditation   85
For prelates of estate,
Their corage to abate
From worldly wantonness,
Their chambers thus to dress
With such parfitness   90
And all such holiness !
Howbeit they let down fall
Their churches cathedráll.

XII

SPEAK PARROT

(Extracts)

I

My name is Parrot, a bird of Paradise,   1
  By nature devised of a wonderous kind,
Daintily dieted with divers delicate spice
  Till Euphrates, that flood, driveth me into Ind ;
  Where men of that country by fortune me find   5
And send me to greate ladyes of estate :
Then Parrot must have an almond or a date.

A cage curiously carven, with a silver pin,
  Properly painted, to be my coverture ;
A mirror of glasse, that I may toot therein :   10
  These maidens full meekly with many a divers flower,
  Freshly they dress, and make sweet my bower,
With ' Speak, Parrot, I pray you ! ' full curtesly they say,
' Parrot is a goodly bird, a pretty popegay.'

With my beak bent, my little wanton eye,   15
  My feathers fresh as is the emerald green,
About my neck a circulet like the rich ruby,
  My little legges, my feet both feat and clean,
  I am a minion to wait upon a queen.
' My proper Parrot, my little pretty fool ! '   20
With ladies I learn, and go with them to school.

---

14 *popegay* parrot. Cf. Ger-   19 *a queen* M. reads " the
man *papagei*, mod. English popin- queen ".
jay.

' Hagh ! Ha ! Ha ! Parrot, ye can laugh prettily ! '
    Parrot hath not dined all this long day.
Like your puss-cat, Parrot can mute and cry
    In Latin, Hebrew, Araby and Chaldy ;   25
    In Greeke tongue Parrot can both speak and say,
As Persius, that poet, doth report of me,
Quis expedivit psittaco suum chaire ?

Douce French of Paris Parrot can learne,
    Pronouncing my purpose after my property,   30
With ' Perliez byen, Parrot, ou perlez rien ! '
    With Dutch, with Spanish, my tongue can agree,
    In England to God Parrot can supply :
' Christ save King Henry the Eighth, our royal king,
The red rose in honour to flourish and spring !   35

With Katherine incomparable, our royal queen also,
    That peerless pomegranate, Christ save her noble
        grace ! '
Parrot saves habler Castiliano,
    With fidasso di cosso in Turkey and in Thrace ;
    Vis consilii expers, as teacheth me Horace,   40
Mole ruit sua, whose dictates are pregnant,
Soventez foys, Parrot, en souvenante.

My lady mistress, Dame Philology,
    Gave me a gifte, in my nest when I lay,

---

24 *mute* mew.

28 *Quis expedivit*, etc. "Who
taught Parrot to say ' χαῖρε ' "
(Greek for " hullo "). The line
is from the Prologue to the
Satires of Persius.

31 *Perliez byen, perlez rien*
for *parlez bien, parlez rien.*

33 *supply* pray.

38 *saves habler Castiliano* for

sabe hablar, etc, " can speak
Castilian ".

39 *fidasso di cosso* probably
a corruption of *fidarsi in se stesso,*
" to trust in oneself ".

40, 41 *Vis consilii expers . . .
mole ruit sua* " Strength without
wisdom falls by its own weight ".
Horace, *Odes* III, iv. 65.

42 *soventez foys . . . en souvenante* often within memory.

To learn all language, and it to speak aptėly,   45
  Now pandez mory, wax frantic, some men say,
  Phronesis for Phrenesis may not hold her way.
An almond now for Parrot, delicately drest :
In Salve festa dies, toto there doth best.

Moderata juvant, but toto doth exceed :   50
  Discretion is mother of noble virtues all.
Myden agan in Greekė tongue we read.
  But reason and wit wanteth their provincial
  When wilfulness is vicar general.
Haec res acu tangitur, Parrot, par ma foy :   55
Ticez-vous, Parrot, tenez-vous coy !

II

GALATHEA

Now, Parrot, my sweet bird, speak out yet once again,   1
Set aside all sophism, and speak now true and plain.

PARROT

So many moral matters, and so little used ;
  So much new making, and so mad time spent ;
So much translation into English confused ;   5
  So much noble preaching, and so little amendment ;
  So much consultation, almost to none intent ;
So much provision, and so little wit at need—
Since Deucalion's flood there can no clerkės rede.

---

46 *pandez mory* meaning unknown.

47 *Phronesis* . . . *Phrenesis* intelligence . . . frenzy.

49 *Salve*, etc. Hail, festal day.

50 *Moderata juvant* moderation pleases.

52 *Myden agan* μηδεν ἀγαν =nothing in excess, a famous Greek maxim.

55 *haec res*, etc. this hits the nail on the head.

56 *Ticez* = Taisez ; *Tenez-vous coy* be quiet.

9 *Deucalion* according to classical legend, when Jupiter overwhelmed the earth with a flood, Deucalion, King of Thessaly, and his wife Pyrrha were the only survivors. See Ovid, *Metamorphoses*, I. 8.

So little discretion, and so much reasoning ;   10
   So much hardy dardy, and so little manliness ;
So prodigal expense, and so shameful reckoning ;
   So gorgeous garments, and so much wretchedness ;
   So much portly pride, with purses penniless ;
So much spent before, and so much unpaid behind—   15
Since Deucalion's flood there can no clerkes find.

So much forecasting, and so far an after deal ;
   So much politic prating, and so little standeth in stead;
So little secretness, and so much great counsel ;
   So many bold barons, their hearts as dull as lead ;   20
   So many noble bodies under a daw's head ;
So royal a king as reigneth upon us all—
Since Deucalion's flood was never seen nor shall.

So many complaintes, and so smalle redress ;
   So much calling on, and so small taking heed ;   25
So much loss of merchandise, and so remediless ;
   So little care for the common weal, and so much need ;
   So much doubtful danger, and so little drede ;
So much pride of prelates, so cruel and so keen—
Since Deucalion's flood, I trow, was never seen.   30

So many thieves hanged, and thieves never the less ;
   So much prisonment for matters not worth an haw ;
So much papers wering for right a small excess ;
   So much pillory-pageants under colour of good law ;
   So much turning on the cuck-stool for every gee-
      gaw ;   35
So much mockish making of statutes of array—
Since Deucalion's flood was never, I dare say.

---

31 *so many thieves* for the whole of this passage of Bk. I of Sir T. More's *Utopia* (1515).

33 *papers wering* apparently a punishment in which the victim wore a paper specifying his crime. According to Hall, Wolsey used to inflict it on perjurers.

35 *cuck-stool* cucking stool, chair used to duck disorderly women or expose them to the public.

So brainless calves' heads, so many sheepès tails ;
   So bold a bragging butcher, and flesh sold so dear ;
So many plucked partridges, and so fatte quails ;   40
   So mangy a mastiff cur, the great greyhound's peer ;
   So big a bulk of brow-antlers cabbaged that year ;
So many swannès dead, and so small revel—
Since Deucalion's flood, I trow, no man can tell.

So many truces taken, and so little perfite truth ;   45
   So much belly-joy, and so wasteful banqueting ;
So pinching and sparing, and so little profit groweth ;
   So many hugy houses building, and so small house-
      holding ;
   Such statutes upon diets, such pilling and polling ;
So is all thing wrought wilfully withoute reason and
    skill—   50
Since Deucalion's flood the world was never so ill.

So many vagabonds, so many beggars bold ;
   So much decay of monasteries and of religious places ;
So hot hatred against the Church, and charity so cold ;
   So much of ' my lordès grace,' and in him no graces, 55
   So many hollow hearts, and so double faces ;
So much sanctuary-breaking, and privilege barred—
Since Deucalion's flood was never seen nor lyerd.

So much ragged right of a rammès horn ;
   So rigorous ruling in a prelate specially ;   60
So bold and so bragging, and was so basely born ;
   So lordly in his looks and so disdainously ;
   So fat a maggot, bred of a fleshe-fly ;
Was never such a filthy Gorgon, nor such an epicure.
Since Deucalion's flood, I make thee fast and sure.   65

---

39 *bragging butcher* Wolsey   to Wolsey.
was a butcher's son.   58 *lyerd* learned.
  55 royal form of address used   60 *prelate* Wolsey.

So much privy watching in cold winters' nights ;
  So much searching of losels, and is himself so lewd ;
So much conjurations for elfish mid-day sprites ;
  So many bulls of pardon published and shewed ;   69
  So much crossing and blessing, and him all beshrewed;
Such pole-axes and pillars, such mules trapt with gold—
Since Deucalion's flood in no chronicle is told.

          Dixit, quod Parrot.

        *   *

---

71 *pole-axes and pillars* This seems to refer to the two silver pillars and the four gilt pole-axes which were carried before Wolsey when he went in state through the streets (see Cavendish's *Life of Wolsey*).

XIII

WHY COME YE NOT TO COURT ?

(Extracts)

I

Once yet again   1
Of you I would frain,
Why come ye not to court ?
To whiche court ?
To the kingès court,   5
Or to Hampton Court ?
Nay, to the kingès court.
The kingès court
Should have the excellence,
But Hampton Court   10
Hath the preeminence,
And Yorkès Place,
With my lordès grace !
To whose magnificence
Is all the confluence   15
Suits and supplications,
Embassades of all nations.
Straw for Law Canon,
Or for the Law Common,
Or for Law Civil !   20
It shall be as he will.
Stop at Law Tancrete,

---

2 *frain* ask.

6 *Hampton Court* Wolsey's favourite residence.

12 *Yorkès Place* Wolsey's palace as Archbishop of York.

13 *my lordès grace* Wolsey, see p. 102, l. 55 n.

18 *Straw* see p. 37, l. 341 n.

22 *Tancrete* transcription, copy.

An abstract or a concrete,
Be it sour, be it sweet,
His wisdom is so discreet   25
That, in a fume or an heat—
' Warden of the Fleet,
Set him fast by the feet ! '
And of his royal power,
When him list to lower,   30
Then, ' Have him to the Tower,
Saunz aulter remedy !
Have him forth, by and by,
To the Marshalsea.
Or to the Kingės Bench ! '   35
He diggeth so in the trench
Of the court royall
That he ruleth them all
So he doth undermind,
And such sleights doth find,   40
That the kingės mind
By him is subverted,
And so straitly coarted
In credencing his tales
That all is but nut-shales   45
That any other saith—
He hath in him such faith.

Now, yet all this might be
Suffered and taken in gre
If that that he wrought   50
To any good end were brought.
But all he bringeth to nought,
By God, that me dear bought !
He beareth the king on hand
That he must pill his land   55

---

32 *saunz aulter* without any.   45 *shales* shells.
43 *coarted* constrained, re-   49 *gre* agreement.
pressed.   55 *pill* pillage.

To make his coffers rich ;
But he layeth all in the ditch,
And useth such abusion
That in the conclusion
All cometh to confusion.   60
He is so ambitious
So shameless, and so vicious,
And so superstitious,
And so much oblivious
From whence that he came   65
That he falleth into a *caeciam*,—
Which, truly to express,
Is a forgetfulness,
Or wilful blindness,
Wherewith the Sodomites   70
Lost their inward sights,
The Gomorrhians also
Were brought to deadly woe,
As Scripture recordes :
A caecitate cordis,   75
(In the Latin sing we)
Libera nos, Domine !

But this mad Amaleck,
Like to a Mamelek,
He regardeth lordès   80
No more than potsherdès !
He is in such elation
Of his exaltation,
And the supportation
Of our sovereign lorde,   85
That, God to recorde,

---

66 *caeciam* blindness.
75–77 *A caecitate cordis*, etc.
"From blindness of heart, O
Lord deliver us".

79 *Mamelek* Mamaluke,
name of Turkish soldiers who
founded a dynasty in Egypt in
the Middle Ages.

He ruleth all at will
Without reason or skill.
Howbeit, the primordial
Of his wretched original,   90
And his base progeny,
And his greasy genealogy,
He came of the sang royall
That was cast out of a butcher's stall.

    But however he was born,   95
Men would have the lesse scorn
If he coulde consider
His birth and roome together,
And call to his minde
How noble and how kinde   100
To him he hath found
Our sovereign lord, chief ground
Of all this prelacy,
That set him nobly
In great authority   105
Out from a low degree,
Which he cannot see.
For he was, pardee,
No doctor of divinity,
Nor doctor of the law,   110
Nor of none other saw ;
But a poore master of art,
God wot, had little part
Of the quatrivials,
Nor yet of trivials,   115
Nor of philosophy,
Nor of philology,
Nor of good policy,
Nor of astronomy,
Nor acquainted worth a fly   120

---

98 *roome* place.   114, 115 *quatrivials, trivials*
medieval university courses.

With honourable Haly.
Nor with royal Ptolemy,
Nor with Albumazar,
To treat of any star
Fixed or else mobile,   125
His Latin tongue doth hobble,
He doth but clout and cobble.
In Tully's faculty
Called humanity.
Yet proudly he dare pretend   130
How no man can him amend.
But have yet not heard this,—
How a one-eyed man is
Well-sighted when
He is among blind men ?   135

II

Should this man of such mood   1
Rule the sword of might
How can he do right ?
For he will as soon smite
His friende as his foe—   5
A proverb long ago.
Set up a wretch on high
In a throne triumphantly,
Make him a great estate,
And he will play checkmate   10
With royal majesty,
Count himself as good as he ;
A prelate potential
To rule under Belial,
As fierce and as cruel   15
As the fiend of hell.

---

128 *Tully*   Cicero.   1   *this man*   Wolsey.

His servants menial
He doth revile, and brawl
Like Mahound in a play ;
No man dare him withsay.	20
He hath despite and scorn
At them that be well-born ;
He rebukes them and rails :
' Ye whoresons !   Ye vassails !
Ye knaves ! Ye churlês sonnes !	25
Ye ribalds, not worth two plummes !
Ye rain-beaten beggars rejagged !
Ye recrayed, ruffians, all ragged !
With ' Stoop, thou havell,
Run, thou javell !	30
Thou peevish pie pecked,
Thou losel long-necked !
Thus, daily, they be decked,
Taunted and checked,
That they are so woe,	35
They wot not whither to go.

---

19 *Mahound* Mahomet, represented in miracle plays as a boastful tyrant.

28 *recrayed* recreant.
29 *havell* low fellow.
30 *javell* worthless fellow.

XIV

From THE GARLAND OF LAUREL

1. TO THE RIGHT NOBLE COUNTESS OF SURREY

After all duly ordered obeisance,   1
  In humble wise as lowly as I may,
Unto you, madame, I make reconusance,
  My life enduring I shall both write and say,
  Recount, report, rehearse without delay   5
The passing bounty of your noble estate,
Of honour and worship which has the former date :

Like to Argiva by just resemblance,
  The noble wife of Polimites king ;
Prudent Rebecca, of whom remembrance   10
  The Bible maketh ; with whose chaste living
  Your noble demeanour is counterweighing,
Whose passing bounty and right noble estate,
Of honour and worship it hath the former date.

The noble Pamphila, queen of the Greekės land,   15
  Habiliments royal found out industriously
Tamar also wrought with her goodly hand
  Many devices passing curiously ;
  Whom ye represent and exemplify.
Whose passing bounty and right noble estate,   20
Of honour and worship it hath the former date.

---

3 *reconusance* acknowledgment, thanks.

8 *Argiva* Argia, wife of Polynices.

9 *Polimites* Polynices, Prince of Thebes.

15 *Pamphila* A Greek woman mentioned by Pliny as famous for her weaving.

17 *Tamar* sister of Absalom, see Samuel ii. 13.

As dame Thamaris, which took the King of Perse,
   Cyrus by name, as writeth the story ;
Dame Agrippina also I may rehearse
   Of gentle courage the parfit memory.   25
   So shall your name endure perpetually,
Whose passing bounty, and right noble estate,
Of honour and worship it hath the former date.

2. TO MISTRESS MARGERY WENTWORTH

      With margerain gentle   1
        The flower of goodlihead,
      Embroidered the mantle
        Is of your maidenhead.
      Plainly I can not glose ;   5
        Ye be, as I divine,
      The pretty primrose,
        The goodly columbine
      With margerain gentle,
        The flower of goodlihead,   10
      Embroidered the mantle
        Is of your maidenhead.
      Benign, courteous, and meek,
        With wordès well devisèd ;
      In you, who list to seek,   15
        Be virtues well comprisèd.
      With margerain gentle
        The flower of goodlihead,
      Embroidered the mantle
        Is of your maidenhead.   20

---

22 *Thamaris* Tomyris, a queen of the Masseyetae, by whom Cyrus, King of Persia, was slain in battle.
24 *Agrippina* daughter of Augustus, mother of Nero.

25 *parfit* perfect.
1 *margerain* marjoram.
5 *glose* flatter.
7 *primrose* the reading of F. ; M. has " primèrose ", which perhaps improves the rhythm.

3. TO MISTRESS ISABEL PENNELL

By saint Mary, my lady,
Your mammy and your daddy
Brought forth a goodly baby ! 1

My maiden Isabell,
Reflaring rosabell,
The flagrant camomell ; 5

The ruddy rosary,
The soverain rosemary,
The pretty strawberry ;

The columbine, the nept, 10
The jeloffer well set,
The proper violet.

Ennewèd your colóur
Is like the daisy flower
After the April shower. 15

Star of the morrow gray,
The blossom on the spray,
The freshest flower of May.

Maidenly demure,
Of womanhood the lure,
Wherefore I make you sure, 20

It were an heavenly health,
It were an endless wealth,
A life for God Himself.

---

5 *Reflaring rosabell* odorous rose-tree.
10 *nept* catmint.

11 *jeloffer* gillyflower, a name for the whole class of carnations, pinks and sweet williams.

To hear this nightingale,   25
Among the birdès smale,
Warbèling in the vale,
Dug, dug,
Jug, jug,
Good year and good luck,   30
With chuk, chuk, chuk, chuk.

4. TO MISTRESS MARGARET HUSSEY

Merry Margaret,   1
    As midsummer flower,
Gentle as falcon
Or hawk of the tower ;
With solace and gladness,   5
Much mirth and no madness,
All good, and no badness,
So joyously,
So maidenly,
So womanly   10
Her demeaning
In every thing,
Far, far passing
That I can endite,
Or suffice to write   15
Of merry Margaret !
As midsummer flower,
Gentle as falcon
Or hawk of the tower ;
As patient and as still   20
And as full of good will
As fair Isaphill ;
Colyander,

---

4 *tower* in the sense of "lofty flight, soaring" (*N.E.D.*).
22 *Isaphill* Hypsipyle, queen of Lemnos, wife of Jason.

23 *Colyander* Middle English form of Coriander, a plant with aromatic fruit used for flavouring.

Sweet pomander,
Good Cassander ;   25
Steadfast of thought,
Well made, well wrought ;
Far may be sought
Erst that ye can find
So courteous, so kind   30
As merry Margaret,
This midsummer flower,
Gentle as falcon,
Or hawk of the tower.

5. TO MISTRESS ISABEL KNIGHT

But if I should acquit your kindness,   1
    Else say ye might
That in me were great blindness
I for to be so mindless,
    And could not write   5
    Of Isabel Knight.

It is not my custom or my guise
    To leave behind
Her that is noth womanly and wise,
And specially which glad was to devise   10
    The means to find,
    To please my mind,

In helping to work my laurel green
    With silk and gold :
Galatea, the maid well beseen,   15
Was never half so fair I ween,
    Which was extolled,
    A thousand fold

---

24 *pomander* a composition
of perfumes in the shape of a ball
sometimes worn about the neck.
25 *Cassander* Cassandra,

Trojan princess and prophetess,
daughter of Priam.
15 *Galatea* See Virgil, *Ecl.*
I and III.

By Maro, the Mantuan prudent,
  Who list to read :   20
But, and I had leisure competent,
I could show you such a precedent
  In very deed
  How ye exceed :

---

19   *Maro*   Virgil.

XV

HOW THE DOUGHTY

DUKE OF ALBANY

LIKE A COWARD KNIGHT, RAN AWAY SHAME-FULLY WITH AN HUNDRED TRATLING SCOTS AND FAINT-HEARTED FRENCHMEN, BESIDE THE WATER OF TWEED.

(Extract)

Rejoice, England,   1
And understand
These tidings new,
Which be as true
As the gospell.   5
This duke so fell
Of Albany,
So cowardly,
With all his host
Of the Scottish coast,   10
For all their boast,
Fled like a beast ;
Wherefore to jest
Is my delight
Of this coward knight,   15
And for to write
In the despite
Of the Scottès rank
Of Huntly-bank,

Title The Scottish Duke of Albany with a mixed Scottish and French army invaded the English border country in 1532, but was driven back by English forces under the Earl of Surrey.

Of Lowdyan,   20
Of Locryan,
And the ragged ray
Of Galaway.
   Dunbar, Dundee,
Ye shall trow me,   25
False Scots are ye ;
Your hearts sore fainted,
And so attainted,
Like cowards stark,
At the castle of Wark,   30
By the water of Tweed,
Ye had evil speed ;
Like cankered curs
Ye lost your spurs,
For in that fray   35
Ye ran away,
With, hey, dog, hey !

For Sir William Lyle
Within short while,
That valiant knight,   40
Put you to flight ;
By his valiance
Two thousand of France
There he put back,
To your great lack,   45
And utter shame
Of your Scottish name.
Your chief chieftain,
Void of all brain,
Duke of all Albany,   50
Then shamefully

---

20 *Lowdyan* Lothian.   38 *Sir William Lyle* Cap-
21 *Locryan* Loch Ryan.   tain of the castle of Wark.

He reculèd back,
To his great lack,
When he heard tell
That my lord Admiral   55
Was coming down
To make him frown
And to make him lour,
With the noble power
Of my lord Cardinal,   60
As an host royall,
After the ancient manner,
With Saint Cuthbert's banner,
And Saint William's alsó ;
Your capitain ran to go,   65
To go, to go, to go,
And brake up all his host ;
For all his crake and boast,
Like a coward knight
He fled and durst not fight,   70
He ran away by night.

---

52 *reculèd* recoiled.
55 *lord Admiral* The Earl
of Surrey, Skelton's patron,
father of the poet Henry Howard,
Earl of Surrey.

XVI

A DEFENCE OF POETRY

(Extract from *A Replication against Certain Young Scholars
abjured of late*)

Why have ye then disdain   1
At poets, and complain
How poets do but feign ?

    Ye do much great outrage
For to disparage   5
And to discourage
The fame matriculate
Of poets laureate.
    For if ye sadly look,
And wisely read the Book   10
Of Good Advertisement,
With me ye must consent
And infallibly agree
Of necessity,
How there is a spirituall,   15
And a mysteriall,
And a mysticall,
Effect energiall,
As Greekès do it call,
Of such an industry.   20
And such a pregnancy,
Of heavenly inspiration
In laureate creation,
Of poets' commendation,
That of divine miseration   25
God maketh his habitation

---

11   *Good Advertisement*   a lost work of Skelton.

In poets which excells,
And sojourns with them and dwells.

By whose inflammation
Of spiritual instigation   30
And divine inspiration
We are kindled in such fashion
With heat of the Holy Ghost,
Which is God of mightès most
That he our pen doth lead,   35
And maketh in us such speed
That forthwith we must need
With pen and ink proceed,
Sometime for affection,
Sometime for sad direction,   40
Sometime for correction,
Sometime under protection
Of patient sufferance,
With sober circumstance,
Our mindes to advance   45
To no man's annoyance ;
Therefore no grievance,
I pray you, for to take
In this that I do make
Against these frenetics,   50
Against these lunatics,
Against these schismatics,
Against these heretics,
Now of late abjurèd,
Most unhappily urèd :   55
For be ye well-assurèd
That frenzy, nor jealousy
Nor heresy will never die.

SELECT BIBLIOGRAPHY

1. TEXTS

(The capital letters beside the first six items are for reference in the footnotes)

F   A right delectable treatyse upon a goodly garland or chapelet of Laurell by Mayster Skelton Poet laureate studyously dyvysed at Sheryfhotton Castell . . . (colophon) Imprynted by me Richarde faukes dwellydg in dura rent or else in Powlis chyrche yarde at the sygne of the A.B.C. The yere of our lorde god MCCCCCxxiij The iij day of Octobre (1523).

R   Magnyfycence a goodly Interlude and a mery devysed and made by Mayster Skelton poete laureate late deceasyd Printed by John Rastell (1533).

L   Hereafter foloweth certayne bokes cŏpyled by mayster Skelton Poet Laureat whose names here after shall appere . . . Printed at London by Richard Lant for Henry Tab dwelling in Pauls churchyard at the sygne of Judith (1545).

K   Hereafter foloweth a litel boke called Colyn Cloute compyled by mayster Skelton Poete Laureate . . . (colophon) Imprinted at London by me Rycharde Kele dwellyng in the powltry at the long shop under saynt Myldredes churche (? C. 1550).

M   Pithy pleasaunt and profitable workes of maister Skelton Poet Laureate Nowe collected and newly published ANNO 1568. Imprinted at London in Fletestreate, neare unto Saint Dunstones churche by Thomas Marsh.

D   The Poetical Works of John Skelton with Notes and
Some Account of the Author and his Writings by
the Rev. Alexander Dyce in two volumes. . . . London
MDCCCXLIII.

The Complete Poems of John Skelton Poet Laureate.
Edited by Philip Henderson, London and Toronto,
J. M. Dent and Sons Ltd.   (1st ed. 1931, 2nd revised ed.
1948.   Modernized text.)

2. CRITICISM AND BIOGRAPHY

Elizabeth Barrett Browning :   *The Book of the Poets* (vol. IV
of *Poetical Works*, 1866).   These essays were originally
printed in the *Athenaeum* in 1842 and were reprinted with
essays on *The Greek Christian Poets* in 1863)

J. M. Berdan : *Early Tudor Poetry*, New York, 1920

E. Blunden : " John Skelton " in *Votive Tablets*, London,
1931

W. H. Auden : " John Skelton " in *The Great Tudors*, ed. K.
Garvin, London, 1935

L. J. Lloyd : *John Skelton*, Oxford, 1936

Ian Gordon : *John Skelton Poet Laureate*, Melbourne and
London, 1943.

INDEX OF WORDS
EXPLAINED IN THE NOTES

(References are to pages on which words occur for the first time and
are explained in the footnotes)

A

Agrippina, 111
Agrise, 39
Albumazer, 60
Alcaeus, 69
Alecto, 46
Amice, 62
Anchor, 91
And, 26
Antiochus, 68
Appose, 90
Aquilonis (princes), 92
Argiva, 110
Armony, 52
Ascry, 92
At a braid, 31
At nale, 38

B

Bale (of dice), 39
Bale (misfortune), 85
Barbed, 83
Barnacle, 58
Baudeth, 75
Bede-rolls, 44
Begared, 91
Belimmed, 35
Bess, Lady.   *See* Elizabeth
Bewray, 33
Birle, 76
Bitter, 58
Ble, 81
Blo, 22
Bloder, 90
Bob me on the noll, 34
Bobbed, 23
Bone aventure, 28
Bonne, 83
Boot, 85

Bootless, 19
Bote, 35
Bowge, 25
Brace, 79
Branxton, 78
Breviate, 87
Bridling-cast, 39
Brimly, 81
Brinning, 19
Bristow, 74
Bussed, 85
Bydene, 96

C

Cam, 52
Camock, 81
Camously, 73
Card of ten.   *See* Outface
Carlish, 53
Carow, 44
Cassander, 114
Catacumbas of Cayre, 81
Catywade, captain of, 80
Celestine, 27
Chaffer, 28
Cherry fair, 16
Chesten, Sir, 80
Chevisaunce, 28
Clergy, 90
Coarted, 105
Cockwats, 31
Coe, 59
Colyander, 113
Comerous, 35
Coney, 75
Conning, 30
Conning bag, 89
Contribute, 16
Countering, 59
Crake (crack), 22

Crake (vaunt), 79
Cross, 95
Crowch, 38
Cuck-stool, 101
Cut, keep his, 48

D

Danger, 27
Daw, 86
Dawcock, Doctor, 36
Dawes, Johan, 35
Demy, 38
Dennes, 47
Deucalion, 100
Dine, 19
Diriges, 94
Discure, 33
Disguised, 37
Divendop, 58
Doom, 49
Douglas, Sir, 80
Dread, 39
Dress, 25
Dressed, 26
Drevil, 37

E

Egyptian, 74
Elizabeth, Queen (wife of Edward IV), 17
Eltham, 16
Encheason, 22
Estridge, 59
Evander, 68

F

Farly, 84
Favell, 29
Fell, 18
Ferumbras, Sir, 81
Fet, 62
Flocket, 73
Francis, St. of Assisi, 41

Fraunchise, 19
Freat, 46
Freke, 81
Frollo de Franko, 80

G

Galatea, 114
Gant, 58
Garded 38
Garred, 85
Gaynour, 65
Gerfawcon, 62
Getes, 74
Gil, 92
Gill, 72
Girn, 80
Glair, 73
Glee, 85
Glent, 83
Glome, 28
Glose, 111
Glum, 95
Good Advertisement, Book of, 119
Gore, 55
Gowny, 73
Grail, 58
Gre, 105
Gressop, 48
Gryll, 72

H

Haft, 43
Haine, 36
Haly, 60
Hampton Court, 104
Harvey Hafter, 30
Harvest girdle, 76
Haut, 90
Havell, 109
Haw, 86
Hawtie, 35
Heckle, 76
Hermoniac, 91
Hight, 84

Hobby, 62
Hoder moder, 90
Howard, Henry, 118
Huckles, 73

I

I chill, 72
Imperiall, 15
Isaphill, 113

J

Jack of the Noke, 92
Jagging, 86
Japhet, 52
Javell, 109
Jeloffer, 112
Jemmy (James IV), 78
Jet, 73
Jetty, 73
Jolly fet, 73
Josephus, 68

K

Kirby Kendal, 38
Kithed, 80
Kuss, 55
Kyrie, Eleison, 56

L

Lacrymable, 18
Lege de moy, 96
Lanners, 62
Leare, 72
Lemster, 75
Lene, 28
Let, 85
Libany, 53
Libius, Sir, 81
Linde, 33
Linus, 69

List (*like*), 23
List (*border*), 38
Locryan, 117
'long, 41
Losel, 84
Lowdyan, 117
Luge, 87
Lurden, 85
Lusk, 81
Lybius Disconius, 65
Lycaon, 54
Lyerd, 102
Lyle, Sir William, 117

M

Mahound, 109
Male, 67
Mamelek, 106
Manticors, 53
Mantrible, 81
Marcellus, Marcus, 68
Mardocheus, 68
Marees, 46
Margerain, 111
Maro, 115
Mavis, 57
Medusa, 46
Meed, 84
Megaera, 46
Melanchates, 53
Mell, 19
Menander, 58
Merlions, 62
Mitre, 91
Mood, in, 36
Mowed, 22
Mur, 57
Murrion, 81
Musket, 62
Muss, 55
Mute, 99

N

Nall, 80
Nayed, 22
Nept, 112

Nobles, 42
Nones Black, 44

Quatrivials, 107
Quintine, Saint, 42
Quod, 21

O

Orcady, 54
Orwell, 81
Ouche, 66
Outface him with a card of ten, 36
Out of harre, 86
Outray, 47

R

Race, 23
Reboke, 31
Reconusance, 110
Recrayed, 109
Reculed, 118
Rede, 84
Redes, 93
Reflare, 61
Reflaring, 112
Reke, 31
Ribskin, 77
Rochets, 91
Rock, 76
Rocket, 73
Rood, 76
Roome, 107
Ropy, 72
Rosabell, 112
Rued, 45

P

Paid, 93
Pamphila, 110
Papers wering, 101
Paramour, 21
Parfit, 111
Paris and Vienne, 65
Pater noster, 44
Patlet, 85
Pay, 21
Pek, 57
Peketh, 88
Pergame, 50
Pherecydes, 69
Pill, 105
Pistell, 57
Plenarly, 32
Pluck, 38
Poke, 31
Polimites, 110
Pomander, 114
Popegay, 98
Popingay, 57
Porsena, 68
Poules, 92
Pounsed, 42
Powers Key, 26
Ptolomy, 60

S

Sacre, 62
Sain, 72
Salt, 75
Satrapas, Sir, 80
Sauncepere, 26
Saunz aulter, 105
Sautes, 87
Scot, 76
Sedean, 62
Shales, 105
Shem, 52
Shidered, 18
Shoder, 90
Shrive, 32
Side, 40
Simonac, 91
Simper the cocket, 74
Sith, 15
Skillet, 75
Slaty, 75

Q

Quaire, 79
Quater Fils Aymon, 65
Quater trey dews, 37

Slo, 86
Snite, 57
Somedele, 73
Sow, 74
Spair, 55
Spink, 57
Stale, 21
Stopping oyster, 41
Stound, 45
Stour, 78
Straw, 37
Sulpicia, 49
Surrey, Earl of, 118

T

Tabards, 91
Tamar, 110
Tancrete, 104
Tarsel gentil, 62
Tattershall, 16
Teder, 41
Tegs, 81
Ten, card of. *See* Outface
Termagant, 80
Terry, Sir, 80
Thamaris, 111
Thomas, Saint, of Kent, 37
Thurification, 61
Titivels, 93
T'oder, 90
Toot, 57
Tower, 113
Tratling, 78
Traves, 27
Trim-tram, 74
Trivials, 107
Troilus, 66

Trowed, 27
Tully, 108
Tyburn, 39

U

Unneth, 45

V

Vesca, 68
Versing-box, 33
Vilyard, 84
Virtue, 40

W

Wanhope, 87
Wark, 62
Ween, 41
Wete, 50
Wharrow, 77
Whinyard, 38
Widered, 18
Windsor, 17
Wood, 36
Woodhack, 57
Wookes, 84
Worrowed, 45
Wyte, 25

Z

Zenophontes, 47

83
85